George William Frederick Howard Carlisle

Lectures and Addresses in Aid of Popular Education

Including a Lecture on the Poetry of Pope

George William Frederick Howard Carlisle

Lectures and Addresses in Aid of Popular Education
Including a Lecture on the Poetry of Pope

ISBN/EAN: 9783744670449

Printed in Europe, USA, Canada, Australia, Japan

Cover: Foto ©ninafisch / pixelio.de

More available books at **www.hansebooks.com**

LECTURES AND ADDRESSES

IN AID OF

POPULAR EDUCATION

INCLUDING

A LECTURE ON THE POETRY OF POPE

BY

THE RIGHT HONOURABLE
THE EARL OF CARLISLE

NEW EDITION

LONDON
LONGMAN, GREEN, LONGMAN, AND ROBERTS
1862

ADVERTISEMENT.

THIS collection of LECTURES and ADDRESSES, delivered by the Earl of Carlisle before Mechanics' Institutions and other Societies of a like nature, is published, with his Lordship's permission, by the Committee of the "Yorkshire Union of Mechanics' Institutes."

In Yorkshire, this valuable class of institutions has flourished more than in any other part of the kingdom, owing, in a considerable measure, to the existence of a "Union" which now comprises 120 Institutes, containing about 20,000 members. Of that "Union," and of many of the individual Institutes, the Earl of Carlisle has been one of the earliest, most constant, and most generous friends; he gave them his high sanction and active assistance whilst Member for the West Riding, and did not withdraw it after his removal from the Lower to the Upper House of Parliament.

The LECTURES on "The Poetry of Pope" and on his Lordship's "Travels in America" were spontaneously offered by the Noble Earl to the Mechanics' Institution and Literary Society of Leeds, as the central Institution of Yorkshire, and were delivered to crowded and admiring audiences. The manuscript being presented to the Committee of the "Yorkshire Union," they were published in a cheap form, and many thousand copies were circulated among the Institutes of that and the neighbouring counties. They have also been published in various and large impressions in the United States.

ADVERTISEMENT.

The ADDRESSES now collected were delivered, in the order of their appearance, before several Institutions, including, besides Mechanics' Institutes, the Huddersfield College, the Manchester and Sheffield Athenæums, and the associated Sunday Schools of Halifax. They are reprinted from the newspaper reports, taken at the time; but the Noble Author has kindly taken the trouble of correcting them.

In their collected form, these Lectures and Addresses exhibit the zealous efforts of a public man, high in rank and in office, for the intellectual entertainment and moral improvement of the humbler classes of his fellow countrymen. Whilst they inform and delight the reader, may they exercise a yet higher influence; may the example of Lord Carlisle induce many men of eminent station and attainments to lend their aid to the multitudes who are seeking the means of self-improvement; and thus may the different classes of society be bound together in mutual good will, and the whole mass be leavened with knowledge, virtue, and religion!

CONTENTS.

LECTURES.

	Page
I. On the Poetry of Pope	7
II. On the Earl of Carlisle's Travels in America	32

ADDRESSES.

On the Benefits conferred by Education: at the Distribution of Prizes at Huddersfield College, December, 1843 - - - 70

On the Utility of Mechanics' Institutes: at the Yorkshire Union of Mechanics' Institutes, held at Wakefield, May, 1844 - - - 73

On the Leeds Mechanics' Institute: February, 1845 - - 77

On Sunday School Instruction: at the Halifax Sunday School Jubilee, June, 1846 - - - - - - 83

On the high Position attained by the Mechanics' Institutes of Yorkshire: at the Yorkshire Union of Mechanics' Institutes, held at Huddersfield, June, 1846 - - - - 88

On the Bradford Mechanics' Institute: October 6, 1846 - - 95

On the Manchester Athenæum: October, 1846 - - - 102

On the Union of Labour and Intellectual Attainments: at the Sheffield Athenæum, September, 1847 - - - - 108

On the real Objects of Mechanics' Institutes: at the Yorkshire Union of Mechanics' Institutes, held at Hull, June, 1848 - 112

On the Great Exhibition of 1851: at the Yorkshire Union of Mechanics' Institutes, held at Leeds, June, 1851 - - - - 117

On the Improvement and Development of the Intellect: at the Mechanics' Institute, Lincoln, October, 1851 - - - - 121

On the Opening of a New Hall at Burnley Mechanics' Institute: November, 1851 - - - - - - 125

LECTURES AND ADDRESSES.

LECTURE I.

ON THE POETRY OF POPE.

I HAVE undertaken to read a paper on "The Poetry of Pope." My hearers, however, will be sorely disappointed, and my own purpose will have been singularly misconstrued, if any expectation should exist that I am about to bring any fresh matter or information to the subject with which I am about to deal. Such means of illustration, I trust, may be amply supplied by Mr. Croker, who has announced a new edition of Pope,— a task for which both his ability and his long habits of research appear well to qualify him. As little is it within either my purpose or my power to present you with any novelty of view, or originality of theory, either upon poetry in general, or the poetry of Pope in particular. The task that I have ventured, perhaps rashly, to impose upon myself, has a much more simple, and, I am willing to hope, less personal aim.

It is briefly this. It has seemed to me for a very long time, — I should say from about the period of my own early youth, — that the character and reputation of Pope, as a poet, had sunk, in general cotemporary estimation, considerably below their previous and their proper level. I felt ruffled at this, as an injustice to an author whom my childhood had been taught to admire, and whom the verdict of my maturer reason approved. I lamented this, because I thought that the extent of this depreciation on the one side, and of the preferences which it necessarily produced on the other, must have a tendency to mislead the public taste, and to misdirect the powers of our rising minstrels.

I allow myself the satisfaction of thinking, that there are already manifest some symptoms of that re-action, which, whenever real merit or essential truth is concerned, will always ensue upon unmerited depression. I remember that it gave me quite a refreshing sensation to find, during my travels in the United States of America, that among some of the most literary and cultivated portions of that great community, (although I would not more implicitly trust to young America than I would to young England upon this point), the reverence for Pope still partook largely of the sounder original faith of the parent land. I fear, however, that there is still enough of heresy extant among us, to justify one who considers himself a true worshipper, who almost bows to the claim of this form of Popish infallibility, in making such efforts as may be within his power to win back any doubtful or hesitating votary to the abandoned shrine.

The attitude, then, in which I appear before you on the present occasion, is this. I look on myself as a counsel, self-constituted it is true, but for whose sincerity the absence of any fee may be considered as a sufficient guarantee; and here, then, in the short space which can be allowed by this Court for the business of the defence, I consider myself bound to put before you such pleas as I may think best calculated to get a verdict from you on my side of the case.

The best plan, which, as it appears to me, I can adopt for disarming any reasonable suspicion on the part of my jurors, (all, I feel sure, candid and enlightened men), as well as for doing justice to my own character as a critic, is to state frankly what I do not claim for my client, the late Alexander Pope. I do not, then, pretend to place him on the very highest pedestal of poetry, among the few foremost of the tuneful monarchs and lawgivers of mankind. Confining ourselves to our own country, I do not, of course, ask you to put him on a level with the universal, undisputed, unassailable, supremacy of Shakspeare — nor with Milton, of whom Mr. Macaulay has lately thus beautifully spoken : —

"A mightier spirit, unsubdued by pain, danger, poverty, obloquy, and blindness, meditated, undisturbed by the obscene tumult which raged all around, a song so sublime and so holy, that it could not have misbecome the lips of those ethereal beings whom he saw, with that inner eye which no calamity could darken, flinging down on the jasper pavement their crowns of amaranth and gold."

I fancy that some might wish to make a further reserve for the gentle fancy of Spenser, though the obsolete character of much of his phraseology, and the tediousness inseparable from all forms of sustained allegory, must, I apprehend, in these days, very considerably contract the number of his readers. Nay, I can quite allow for the preference being given to Pope's more immediate predecessor, Dryden, whose compositions, though certainly less finished and complete, undoubtedly exhibit a more nervous vein of argumentative power, and a greater variety of musical rhythm. When I have mentioned these august names, I have mentioned all, writing in the English tongue, who, in my humble apprehension, can possibly be classed before Pope.

I may observe, that in this estimate I appear to be confirmed by the present Commissioners of Fine Arts, who, in selecting the Poets from whose works subjects for six vacant spaces in the new Palace of Westminster were to be executed by living artists, named Chaucer, (who by his antiquity as well as his merits was properly appointed to lead the line of English bards), Shakspeare, Spenser, Milton, Dryden, and Pope.

Though I conceive, and you will readily concur, that the case I am endeavouring to make good must be mainly established by my client's own precise words, — and the anticipated pleasure of quoting them to attentive ears has been, perhaps, my chief inducement to undertake the office which I am now fulfilling, — yet I consider it will not be out of place for the object I have in view, especially before an audience of a nation which much delights in, and is indeed much ruled by, precedent, if I should quote a few approved authorities, (had time permitted I might have availed myself of a great number), merely for the purpose of showing that if you should be pleased to side with me in this issue, we shall find ourselves in company of which we shall have no need to be ashamed.

I shall also thus furnish a proof of what I have stated above, that I am not straining after originality or novelty of remark; indeed, I feel that I shall make way in proportion as the testimony I adduce proceeds from lips more trustworthy than my own.

What says Savage, a poet himself of irregular but no mean genius? He thus speaks of Pope: —

> " Though gay as mirth, as curious thought sedate,
> As elegance polite, as power elate,

> Profound as reason, and as justice clear,
> Soft as persuasion, yet as truth severe,
> As bounty copious, as persuasion sweet,
> Like nature various, and like art complete:
> So fine her morals, so sublime her views,
> His life is almost equalled by his muse."

Part of this commendation, I must admit, appears even to me overstrained. Some of Pope's compositions are marred by occasional coarseness and indelicacy, and his mind and character, I fear it must be allowed, were at times disfigured by envy, resentment, and littleness. Compared, however, with most of his predecessors of the reign of Charles II., and with many of his own cotemporaries, both his muse and his life may have been deemed decent and severe. He seems himself, at all events, to have indulged in this estimate of the tenor of his own productions:—

> "Curst be the verse, how well soe'er it flow,
> That tends to make one worthy man my foe,
> Give virtue scandal, innocence a fear,
> Or from the soft-eyed virgin steal a tear."

I return to my authorities.

I do not quote Bishop Warburton, as he was the avowed apologist, as well as executor and editor, of Pope.

Dr. Joseph Warton, who wrote an essay on the genius and writings of Pope, chiefly with a view of proving what I have admitted above, that he ought not to be ranked in the highest class of poets, and who appears to wish, as I certainly do not, to have a hit at him whenever he can, concedes, however, thus much to him:—

"In the species of poetry wherein Pope excelled, he is superior to all mankind, and I only say that this species of poetry is not the most excellent one of the art. He is the great poet of reason, the first of ethical authors in verse."

Dr. Johnson, in his well-known and most agreeable "Life of Pope," says thus:—

"Of his intellectual character, the constituent and fundamental principle was good sense;" and then, "Pope had likewise genius, a mind active, ambitious, and adventurous, always investigating, always aspiring, in its widest searches longing to go forward, in its highest flights still wishing to be higher."

And at the close of the masterly contrast which he draws between Dryden and Pope, he thus sums it up: —

"If the flights of Dryden are higher, Pope continues longer on the wing; if of Dryden's fire the blaze is brighter, of Pope is the heat more regular and constant. Dryden often surpasses expectation, and Pope never falls below it; Dryden is read with frequent astonishment, and Pope with perpetual delight."

Mason, also a poet and very accomplished man, who had done so much in editing and illustrating the works of another most eminent and admirable master of his art (I refer to Gray), has shown what an exalted estimate he had formed of Pope, in the passage where he reproaches him for the undue praise which he had lavished on the famous Henry St. John, Viscount Bolingbroke: —

"Call we the shade of Pope from that blest bower,
  Where throned he sits with many a tuneful sage;
Ask, if he ne'er repents that luckless hour,
  When St. John's name illumined glory's page.

Ask, if the wretch who dared his honour stain,
  Ask, if his country's, his religion's foe,
Deserved the wreath that Marlboro' failed to gain,
  The deathless meed, he only could bestow?"

George, Lord Lyttelton, another poet himself, calls him "The sweetest and most elegant of English poets, the severest chastiser of vice, and the most persuasive teacher of wisdom."

How speaks Campbell, the author of "The Pleasures of Hope," and "The Battle of the Baltic"? If any one is entitled to speak of what true poetry is, that right will not be denied to Thomas Campbell. He calls Pope "a genuine poet," and says with true discrimination: —

"The public ear was long fatigued with repetitions of his manner; but if we place ourselves in the situation of those to whom his brilliancy, succinctness, and animation were wholly new, we cannot wonder at their being captivated to the fondest admiration."

I will only further cite from the poets whom many of us remember in our own day, one still more illustrious name. The fervid, wayward, irregular, muse of Lord Byron, presented the strongest points of contrast with the measured, even, highly-trained, smoothly-polished, temperament of Pope. What did Lord Byron think of Pope? He terms him, "The most perfect and harmonious of poets — he, who, having no fault, has had reason made his reproach. It is this very harmony which has raised the vulgar and atrocious cant against him — (Lord Byron was fond of using strong language): — because his versification is perfect, it is assumed that it is his only perfection; because his truths are so clear, it is asserted that he has no invention; and because he is always intelligible, it is taken for granted that he has no genius. I have loved and honoured the fame and name of that illustrious and unrivalled man, far more than my own paltry renown, and the trashy jingle of that crowd of schools and upstarts who pretend to rival or even surpass him. Sooner than a single leaf should be torn from his laurel, it were better that all which these men, and that I, as one of their set, have ever written, should line trunks."

There is another and more general testimony to the reputation, at least, if not to the actual merits of Pope, which may be here mentioned; this is, the extent to which his lines are quoted as familiar maxims and illustrations of the daily incidents of life, and the common meanings of men, — quoted often, probably, by persons who have little knowledge or recollection where the words are to be found. I am inclined to believe that, in this respect, — and it is one not to be considered slightingly, — he would be found to occupy the second place, next, of course, to the universal Shakspeare himself. Allow me to cite a few instances.

When there has been a pleasant party of people, either in a convivial or intellectual view — I wish we might think it of our meeting this evening — we say that it has been —

"The feast of reason, and the flow of soul."

How often are we warned — I have sometimes even heard the warning addressed to Mechanics' Institutes, that —

"A little learning is a dangerous thing."

How often reminded,

"An honest man's the noblest work of God."

Or, with nearly the same meaning,

"Who taught the useful science, to be good."

There is a couplet which I ought to carry in my own recollection —
"What can ennoble sots, or slaves, or cowards?
Alas! not all the blood of all the Howards."

It is an apt illustration of the office of hospitality,
"Welcome the coming, speed the parting guest."

How familiar is the instruction,
"To look, through Nature, up to Nature's God."

As rules with reference to composition,—
"The last and greatest art — the art to blot."
"To snatch a grace beyond the reach of art;"

And then as to the best mode of conveying the instruction,—
"Men must be taught as if you taught them not."

There is the celebrated definition of wit,—
"True wit is nature to advantage dressed;
What oft was thought, but ne'er so well expressed."

Do you want to illustrate the importance of early education? You observe —
"Just as the twig is bent, the tree's inclined."

Do you wish to characterise ambition somewhat favourably? You call it,
"The glorious fault of angels and of gods."

Or describing a great conqueror,—
"A mighty hunter, and his prey was man."

Do you seek the safest rule for architecture or gardening?
"Consult the genius of the place in all;"

Or, with exquisite good sense,
"'Tis use alone that sanctifies expense,
And splendour borrows all her rays from sense."

Are you tempted to say any thing rather severe to your wife or daughter, when she insists on a party of pleasure, or an expensive dress? You tell her,
"That every woman is at heart a rake."

And then if you wish to excuse your own submission, you plead —

> "If to her share some female errors fall,
> Look on her face, and you'll forget them all."

How often are we inclined to echo the truth —

> "For fools rush in where angels fear to tread."

And this too, —

> "That gentle dulness often loves a joke."

Who has not felt this to be true?—

> "Hope springs eternal in the human breast;
> Man never is, but always to be blest."

When an orator, or a Parliamentary candidate — in which last capacity I have often appeared before some of you — wishes to rail at absolute governments, he talks of —

> "The monstrous faith of many made for one."

Then there are two maxims, one in politics and one in religion, which have both been extensively found fault with; but the very amount of censure proves what alone I am now attempting to establish, not the truth or justice of Pope's words, but their great vogue and currency —

> "For forms of government let fools contest;
> Whate'er is best administer'd is best:
> For modes of faith let graceless zealots fight;
> His can't be wrong whose life is in the right."

It is now time to judge Pope from his own works, by which, of course, his place in the estimate of posterity must finally stand.

I shall pass hurriedly by his earlier compositions. He tells us himself of the precocity of his genius:

> "I lisp'd in numbers, for the numbers came."

But his very youthful productions, on the whole, appear to be more remarkable for their dates than their intrinsic merits. He wrote his "Pastorals" at sixteen. Independently of the age at which they were written, they appear to me trivial, forced, out of keeping with the English soil and life to which they are avowedly assigned. One piece of praise is justly their due: after the publication of these verses by a youth—we may call him a boy—of sixteen, I do not see why a rugged or inharmonious English verse need ever again have been written; and what is more, I believe very few such have been written. Mr. Macaulay says on this point, " From the time when the 'Pastorals' appeared, heroic versification became matter of rule and compass, and, before long, all artists were on a level." It was surely better that this level should be one upon which the reader could travel smoothly along, without jolts or stumbles.

In the short poem of the "Messiah," I do justice to the stately flow of verse upon the highest of human themes. Both Dr. Johnson and Dr. Warton give it a decided preference over the "Pollio" of Virgil, which is concerned with topics of close and wonderful similarity. I do not know how far they are right, but I feel quite sure that both the "Pollio" of Virgil and the "Messiah" of Pope fall immeasurably below the prose translation of Isaiah in our Bibles.

"Windsor Forest" appears to be on the whole a cold production. It contains some good lines on the poet Earl of Surrey —

" Matchless his pen, victorious was his lance,
Bold in the lists, and graceful in the dance "—

an extremely pretty account of the flight and plumage of a pheasant, a very poetical list of the tributaries of the Thames, and some well-sounding verses on the Peace of Utrecht, then recently concluded, from which in the early part of this year I was induced to quote some lines which I thought very apposite to the proposed Exhibition of Industry of All Nations, at London, in 1851:—

" The time shall come, when, free as seas or wind,
Unbounded Thames shall flow for all mankind,
Whole nations enter with each swelling tide,
And seas but join the regions they divide ;
Earth's distant ends our glory shall behold,
And the new world launch forth to seek the old."

The Odes written by Pope are decidedly of an inferior caste. I need not say how inferior to the immortal "Ode on St. Cecilia's Day," by Dryden, who preceded — or how inferior to Gray or Campbell, who have followed him. The Ode, perhaps, of every species of poetical composition, was the most alien to the genius of Pope; its character is rapt, vehement, abrupt; his is composed, polished, methodical; his haunt would not be the mountain top or the foaming cataract, but the smooth parterre and the gilded saloon. You may prefer one bent of mind, as you would one form of scenery; the question with which I now invite you to deal is, not in what style Pope wrote, but in the style which he chose, and for which his nature best fitted him, how far he excelled.

Among the very youthful productions of Pope, there were also some adaptations from Chaucer, Ovid, and one or two more ancient authors; in point of execution they are only distinguished by their smooth versification, and the matter of them ought to have forbidden the attempt.

In speaking as I have done of many of Pope's earlier compositions, however I may assume myself to be a devoted admirer — partisan, if you should so please to term it — I conceive that I have at least shown that hitherto I am no indiscriminate praiser, who thinks that everything which proceeds from his favourite must be perfect. On the contrary, though his facility in writing verses was almost precocious, the complete mastery of his art seems to have been gradually and laboriously developed. "So regular my rage," was the description which he has himself applied to his own poetry. It was not so much "the pomp and prodigality of heaven," which have been allotted to a few; it was rather, in the edifice of song which he has reared, that nicety of detail, and that completeness of finish, where every stroke of the hammer tells, and every nail holds its exact place.

His early friend and admirer, Walsh, seems accurately to have discerned the path of excellence which was open for him, when he told him that there was one way in which he might excel any of his predecessors, which was by correctness, for, though we had before him several great poets, we could boast of none that were perfectly correct. Pope justified the advice; and if correctness is not the highest praise to which a poet can aspire, it is no mean distinction to show how an author can be almost faultlessly correct, and almost as invariably the reverse of all that is tame, mean, or flat.

There come, however, among compositions which in any one else would most strictly be called early, a few which will not bear to be dismissed with such a hasty or superficial notice. The "Essay on Criticism" was written when he was twenty or twenty-one years old, and as such it appears a positive marvel. But he had now entered a field on which he was quite a master—the domain of good sense and of good taste, applied to the current literature of a scholar, and the common topics of life.

Very soon after, however, as if to show that, if he had willed it, he could have exercised as full a mastery over the region of light fancy and sportive imagery, as of sober reflection and practical wisdom, he wrote what is termed a heroi-comic poem, the Rape of the Lock. Dr. Johnson calls this the most exquisite example of ludicrous poetry, though I do not think the word ludicrous a happy epithet of the Doctor's; Dr. Warton calls it the best satire extant; and we are told that Pope himself considered the intermixture of the machinery of the Sylphs with the action of the story, as the most successful exertion of his art. As my business to-night is more with Pope on the whole as a poet, than with the details and the conduct of his single poems, I must not suffer myself to linger on the details of this delicious work. It is so finished and nicely fitted together that it would scarcely answer to separate any isolated passages from the context; besides, exquisite as the entire poem is, yet, the subject being professedly trivial, any single extract might appear deficient in importance and dignity. The whole is as sparkling as the jewelled cross upon the bosom of the heroine,—

"On her white breast a sparkling cross she wore,
Which Jews might kiss, and Infidels adore."

It is as stimulating as the pinch of snuff he so compactly describes,

"The pungent grains of titillating dust."

But there was one other chord of the poetic lyre which Pope, still young in years, had yet to show his power to strike, and it is the most thrilling in the whole compass of song—the poetry of the passions and the heart. To this class I assign the Elegy to the Memory of an unfortunate Lady, and the ever memorable Epistle from Eloisa to Abelard. A few words will suffice here for the Elegy; its moral tendency cannot be defended, as it appears, incidentally at least, to excuse and consecrate suicide. In its execution it combines in a high degree poetic diction with pathetic feeling. The concluding lines are most touching:—

> "Poets themselves must fall like those they sung,
> Deaf the praised ear, and mute the tuneful tongue.
> Ev'n he, whose soul now melts in mournful lays,
> Shall shortly want the generous tear he pays;
> Then from his closing eyes thy form shall part,
> And the last pang shall tear thee from his heart,
> Life's idle business at one gasp be o'er,
> The Muse forgot, and thou belov'd no more."

I must pause somewhat longer on the Epistle from Eloisa to Abelard. I ought, however, before I give vent to the full glow of panegyric, to make two admissions; one, that a sensitive delicacy would have avoided the subject; the other, that the matter is not original, but is supplied in great degree by the actual letters of the distinguished and unfortunate pair who gave their names to the epistle. Where the adaptation, however, is so consummate, this makes a very slight deduction from the merit of the author. The poem is not long, but in point of execution it appears to me one of the most faultless of human compositions; every thought is passion, and every line is music. The struggle between aspiring piety and forbidden love forms its basis, and the scenery and accessaries of monastic life and the Roman Catholic ritual furnish a back-ground highly congenial, solemn, and picturesque.

I must endeavour to justify my panegyric by a few quotations. The commendation of letter-writing is well known.

> "Heaven first taught letters for some wretch's aid,
> Some banish'd lover, or some captive maid;
> They live, they speak, they breathe what love inspires,
> Warm from the soul, and faithful to its fires,
> The virgin's wish without her fears impart,
> Excuse the blush, and pour out all the heart,
> Speed the soft intercourse from soul to soul,
> And waft a sigh from Indus to the Pole."

I give the description of the Convent founded by Abelard:—

> "You rais'd these hallow'd walls; the desert smil'd,
> And Paradise was open'd in the Wild.
> No weeping orphan saw his father's stores
> Our shrines irradiate, or emblaze the floors;

> No silver saints, by dying misers given,
> Here brib'd the rage of ill-requited heaven;
> But such plain roofs as piety could raise,
> And only vocal with the Maker's praise."

There is the same scene coloured by Eloisa's own state of mind:—

> "But o'er the twilight groves and dusky caves,
> Long sounding isles, and intermingled graves,
> Black Melancholy sits, and round her throws
> A death-like silence and a dread repose.
> Her gloomy presence saddens all the scene,
> Shades ev'ry flow'r, and darkens ev'ry green,
> Deepens the murmur of the falling floods,
> And breathes a browner horror on the woods."

This is surely eminently poetical and expressive.

Let me give the description of her first acquaintance with Abelard:—

> "Thou know'st how guiltless first I met thy flame,
> When love approach'd me under friendship's name;
> My fancy form'd thee of angelic kind,
> Some emanation of th' all-beauteous Mind.
> Those smiling eyes, attemp'ring every ray,
> Shone sweetly lambent with celestial day.
> Guiltless I gaz'd; heaven listen'd while you sung,
> And truths divine came mended from that tongue."

In that beautiful line, the force of human passion seems to obtain the mastery over the concerns of another life; but I will close my extracts from this poem with the wishes she forms for their last meeting, in which piety appears finally to predominate over passion:—

> "Thou, Abelard! the last sad office pay,
> And smooth my passage to the realms of day.
> See my lips tremble, and my eye-balls roll,
> Suck my last breath, and catch my flying soul!
> Ah no — in sacred vestments may'st thou stand,
> The hallowed taper *trembling* in thy hand.

(You remark all the force in that word "trembling:" in the next line, observe how the words "present" and "lifted" carry on the drama of the scene):—

> *Present* the cross before my *lifted* eye,
> Teach me at once, and learn of me to die.
> Ah then, thy once-lov'd Eloisa see!
> It will be then no crime to gaze on me.

(That is, I think, a highly impassioned and pathetic line.)

> See from my cheek the transient roses fly!

("Transient," in the literal meaning of the word, passing off.)

> See the last sparkle languish in my eye!
> Till every motion, pulse, and breath be o'er;
> And ev'n my Abelard be loved no more.
> O death, all eloquent! you only prove
> What dust we doat on when 'tis man we love."

It would be a strange omission in an estimate of the poetical achievements of Pope, to make no mention of his translation of Homer, though the fact of its being a translation, and its length, would both rather put it beyond the limits of my present criticism. Dr. Johnson calls his Iliad, and I am inclined to believe with no more than perfect truth, the noblest version of poetry which the world has ever seen. The main objection alleged against it is, that being a professed translation of Homer, it is not Homeric,—that it is full of grace and sparkle, but misses the unmatched simplicity and majesty of that great father of verse,—that, if I may so express myself, it has not the twang of Homer. All this, I think, must be admitted; by some the poems of Sir Walter Scott, and old ballads like Chevy Chase, have been thought to convey a better notion of this Homeric twang than can be gathered from all the polished couplets of Pope. Cowper (an honoured name) tried a more literal version in blank verse, which certainly may be said to represent more closely at least the simplicity of the original. Let us, however, come to the practical test—as Lord Byron has asked concerning these two translations, "Who can ever read Cowper, and who will ever lay down Pope, except for the original? As a child I first read Pope's Homer with a rapture which no subsequent work could ever afford, and children are not the worst judges of their own language." It is no mean praise that it is the channel which has conveyed the knowledge of Homer to the general English public,—not to our scholars, of course. Though it is far less to the purpose how I felt about this as a child, than how Lord Byron felt, I too remember the days (I fear, indeed, that the anecdote will savour of egotism, but I must not mind the imputation of egotism, if it illustrates my author,) when I used to learn Pope's Iliad by heart behind a screen, while I was supposed to be engaged on lessons of more direct usefulness; and I fancy that I was under the strange hallucination at the time that I had got by heart the four first books. I do not mention this as a profitable example, but in order to show the degree in which this translation was calculated to gain the mastery over the youthful mind.

All the poems of Pope, to which I have already referred, belong to that period of life which, in all ordinary cases, would be called youth. I believe that they must have been nearly altogether completed before he was thirty. Those which I may further have to quote from (in doing which I shall hardly think it necessary to observe so much separate order between the different poems as heretofore), were the fruits of his matured years and settled powers. They henceforth fall under one class of composition, that which treats of men, their manners, and their morals; they are comprised under the titles of satires and moral essays. He himself speaks of the bent which his genius now adopted,

" That not in fancy's maze he wander'd long,
But stoop'd to truth, and moraliz'd his song."

Upon which I again feel happy to find myself in full acquiescence with Lord Byron, who says, " He should have written, *rose* to truth. In my mind the highest of all poetry is ethical poetry, as the highest of all earthly subjects must be moral truth."

Lord Bolingbroke and Bishop Atterbury, certainly no mean judges of intellectual merit, declared that the strength of Pope's genius lay eminently and peculiarly in satire. What shall I, then, single out as an illustration of his satiric vein? The character of Lord Hervey, under the name of Sporus, is cited by Lord Byron as a specimen of his rich fancy, (generally, but most erroneously, assumed to be the quality in which Pope was chiefly deficient,) and with this specimen of fancy Lord Byron defied all his own cotemporaries to compete. That it does manifest injustice at least to the abilities of Lord Hervey, will be acknowledged by all who have read his very entertaining memoirs lately published; but moreover, able and brilliant as it is, it is too disagreeable to repeat. Let me quote, then, his famous character of Addison, who had given offence to him, whether with good reason or not it is no part of my present purpose, nor would it be in my power, to decide. Pope thought that Addison had treated him slightingly and superciliously, and I believe took specially amiss the kind of notice he had bestowed upon the Rape of the Lock. He speaks of him under the name of Atticus; you will remark the consummate skill with which he first does justice to his genius, and then detracts from its lustre. It is also a great proof of the cleverness of the satire, that, sincere as our respect is both for the genius and character of Addison, it is impossible to go through this piece of dissection without believing that it must have touched upon some points of real soreness.

> "Peace to all such! but were there one whose fires
> True genius kindles, and fair fame inspires;
> Blest with each talent and each art to please,
> And born to write, converse, and live with ease:
> Should such a man, too fond to rule alone,
> Bear, like the Turk, no brother near the throne,
> View him with scornful, yet with jealous eyes,
> And hate for arts that caus'd himself to rise;
> Damn with faint praise, assent with civil leer,
> And without sneering, teach the rest to sneer;
> Willing to wound, and yet afraid to strike,
> Just hint a fault, and hesitate dislike;
> Alike reserv'd to blame or to commend,
> A tim'rous foe, and a suspicious friend;
> Dreading ev'n fools, by flatterers besieg'd,
> And so obliging, that he ne'er oblig'd;
> Like Cato, give his little Senate laws,
> And sit attentive to his own applause;
> While wits and templars every sentence raise,
> And wonder with a foolish face of praise —
> Who but must laugh, if such a man there be?
> Who would not weep, if Atticus were he!"

Then I will take the character of the able, versatile, and unprincipled Duke of Wharton: —

"Wharton, the scorn and wonder of our days,
Whose ruling passion was the lust of praise:
Born with whate'er could win it from the wise,
Women and fools must like him, or he dies;
Tho' wondering senates hung on all he spoke,
The club must hail him master of the joke.

(This couplet has been applied to the celebrated Mr. Sheridan, and does not ill suit the author of the speeches on Warren Hastings's trial, and the School for Scandal.)

Thus with each gift of nature and of art,
And wanting nothing but an honest heart;
Grown all to all, from no one vice exempt;
And most contemptible to shun contempt;
His passion still, to covet general praise,
His life, to forfeit it a thousand ways;
A constant bounty which no friend has made;
An angel tongue, which no man can persuade;
A fool, with more of wit than half mankind;
Too rash for thought, for action too refin'd;
A tyrant to the wife his heart approves;
A rebel to the very king he loves;
He dies, sad outcast of each church and state,
And, harder still! flagitious, yet not great.
Ask you why Wharton broke thro' every rule?
'Twas all for fear the knaves should call him fool."

I have given the characters of two men; fairness demands that at least I should give you one of a woman. I take that of Chloe; most of us will feel that we have known people, to whom some parts of it at least might fit:—

"Yet Chloe sure was form'd without a spot.—
Nature in her then err'd not, but forgot.
'With ev'ry pleasing, ev'ry prudent part,
'Say, what does Chloe want?' She wants a heart.
She speaks, behaves, and acts just as she ought;
But never, never reach'd one generous thought.
Virtue she finds too painful an endeavour,
Content to dwell in decencies for ever.

> So very reasonable, so unmov'd,
> As never yet to love, or to be lov'd.
> She, while her lover pants upon her breast,
> Can mark the figures on an Indian chest:
> And when she sees her friend in deep despair,
> Observes how much a chintz exceeds mohair.
> Forbid it, heav'n, a favour or a debt
> She e'er should cancel! but she may forget.
> Safe is your secret still in Chloe's ear;
> But none of Chloe's shall you ever hear.
> Of all her Dears she never slander'd one,
> But cares not if a thousand are undone.
> Would Chloe know if you're alive or dead?
> She bids her footman put it in her head.
> Chloe is prudent — Would you too be wise?
> Then never break your heart when Chloe dies."

Having thus attempted to do justice to Pope's powers of satire, I must not omit to mention what I consider to be another of his felicities almost of an opposite character, though I have perceived with pleasure since I noted this topic, that I have been anticipated in the same line of remark by the late Mr. Hazlitt; I say with pleasure, because that ingenious person was one of the guides and favourites of a school the most opposed in theory and practice to that of Pope; I allude to the extreme tact, skill, and delicacy with which he conveys a compliment, and frequently embodies in one pregnant line or couplet a complete panegyric of the character he wishes to distinguish. Let me instance this by a few examples. Sometimes the compliment appears merely to be thrown out almost as it were by chance to illustrate his meaning. So of the Duke of Chandos, whom at another time he is supposed to have intended to ridicule under the character of Timon—

> "Thus gracious Chandos is belov'd at sight."

Then of Lord Cornbury—

> "Would ye be blest? despise low joys, low gains;
> Disdain whatever Cornbury disdains."

Of General Oglethorpe, the founder of Georgia—

> "One driv'n by strong benevolence of soul
> Shall fly, like Oglethorpe, from pole to pole."

These have reference to manly virtues; sometimes there is the same oblique reference to female claims;

"Hence Beauty, waking all her tints, supplies,
An angel's sweetness, or Bridgewater's eyes."

At other times the eulogium is more direct. Take that fine application to Lord Cobham of the effect of man's ruling passion, developing itself in death, which he has been pursuing through a number of instances,—the man of pleasure, the miser, the glutton, the courtier, the coquette, all, for the most part, under circumstances derogatory to the pride of human nature, when he thus sums them up—

"And you, brave Cobham, to the latest breath
Shall feel your ruling passion strong in death;
Such, in those moments, as in all the past,
'Oh, save my country, Heav'n!' shall be your last."

How beautiful is the couplet to Dr. Arbuthnot, his physician and friend—

"Friend to my life! (which did not you prolong,
The world had wanted many an idle song)."

How ingenious that to the famous Philip Stanhope, Earl of Chesterfield, on being desired to write some lines in an album with his pencil—

"Accept a miracle instead of wit,
See two *dull* lines by Stanhope's pencil writ."

How happy is the allusion to Lord Peterborough, who made a brilliant campaign in Spain within a wonderfully short time. He represents him as assisting to lay out his grounds—

"And he whose lightning pierc'd th' Iberian lines
Now forms my quincunx, and now ranks my vines;
Or tames the genius of the stubborn plain,
Almost as quickly as he conquer'd Spain."

He always speaks of Murray, the great Lord Mansfield, with pride and affection. It is true, that one of the worst lines he ever wrote is about him, the second in this couplet—

"Grac'd as thou art, with all the power of words,
So known, so honour'd, at the House of Lords."

An instance how much delicacy it requires to introduce with effect familiar names and things; sometimes it tells with great force; here it is disastrously prosaic; we almost forgive it, however, when he turns from the Palace of Westminster to the Abbey opposite —

"Where Murray, long enough his country's pride,
Shall be no more than Tully, or than Hyde."

He again alludes to the aptitude for poetical composition which Murray had exhibited, and also to the talent for epigram which he assumes that the great orator Pulteney would have displayed if he had not been engrossed by politics.

"How sweet an Ovid, Murray, was our boast;
How many Martials were in Pulteney lost."

These were for the most part his political friends, but when he mentions Sir Robert Walpole, to whom his friends, more than himself, were virulently opposed, how respectful and tender is the reproach, how adroit and insinuating the praise —

"Seen him I have, but in his happier hour,
Of social pleasure, ill exchang'd for power, —
Seen him, uncumber'd with a venal tribe,
Smile without art, and win without a bribe."

I might adduce many other instances; I might quote at full length the noble epistle to Lord Oxford, but I will sum up this topic with that striking passage in which, while he enumerates the persons who encouraged and fostered his earlier productions, he presents us with a gallery of illustrious portraits, sometimes conveys by a single word an insight into their whole character, and concludes the distinguished catalogue with the name of that St. John whom he uniformly regarded with feelings little short of idolatry, and which, however misplaced and ill-grounded, have even in themselves something of the poetical attribute —

"But why then publish? Granville the polite,
And knowing Walsh, would tell me I could write;
Well-natured Garth inflamed with early praise,
And Congreve loved, and Swift endured, my lays;

(Observe how the gentle and amiable Congreve "loved," and the caustic and cynical Swift "endured.")

> The courtly Talbot, Somers, Sheffield, read,
> E'en mitred Rochester would nod the head,

(said to have been the ordinary symptom of Bishop Atterbury being pleased; then comes the swelling climax,)

> And St. John's self, great Dryden's friend before,
> With open arms receiv'd one Poet more,
> Happy my studies, when by these approv'd!
> Happier their author, when by these belov'd!

I feel that I ought not entirely to omit all mention of the long satiric poem of the Dunciad, upon which Pope evidently bestowed much care and labour; but it is throughout disfigured by great ill-nature, and by a pervading run of unpleasant and unsavoury images. There is much spirit in the account of the young high-born Dunce, who makes, what is called, the Grand Tour —

> "Europe he saw, and Europe saw him too;"

and tells how he

> "Judicious drank, and, greatly daring, dined."

There is a luscious kind of burlesque softness in these lines,

> "To happy convents, bosom'd deep in vines,
> Where slumber abbots, purple as their wines;
> To isles of fragrance, lily-silver'd vales,
> Diffusing languor in the panting gales;
> To lands of singing, or of dancing slaves,
> Love-whisp'ring woods, and lute-resounding waves."

One of the most distinguishing excellencies of Pope is the vividness which he imparts to all the pictures he presents to the mind, and which he attains by always making use of the very most appropriate terms which the matter admits. This, in conjunction with his wonderful power of compression, which he has probably carried further than any one before or since, gives a terseness and completeness to all he says, in which he is unrivalled. As instances of this perfect picture painting, I would refer you, as I must not indefinitely indulge in long citations, to the descriptions, all in the same Epistle on Riches, of the Miser's House, the Man of Ross's charities, and of the death of Villiers, Duke of Buckingham:

> "In the worst inn's worst room, with mat half hung,
> The floors of plaister, and the walls of dung,
> On once a flock-bed, but repair'd with straw,
> With tape-tied curtains, never meant to draw,
> The George and Garter dangling from that bed
> Where tawdry yellow strove with dirty red,
> Great Villiers lies — alas! how changed from him,
> That life of pleasure, and that soul of whim!"

If any should object that this is all very finished and elaborate, but it is very minute—only miniature painting after all, what do you say to this one couplet on the operations of the Deity?

> "Builds life on death, on change duration founds,
> And gives the eternal wheels to know their rounds."

I would beg any of the detractors of Pope to furnish me with another couple of lines from any author whatever, which encloses so much sublimity of meaning within such compressed limits, and such precise terms.

I must cite another passage, in which he ventures on the same exalted theme, with somewhat more enlargement; it would be impossible, however, for you to hear it, and bring against it any charge of diffuseness:

> "All are but parts of one stupendous whole,
> Whose body Nature is, and God the soul;
> That, chang'd through all, and yet in all the same,
> Great in the earth, as in the ethereal frame;
> Warms in the sun, refreshes in the breeze,
> Glows in the stars, and blossoms in the trees,
> Lives through all life, extends through all extent,
> Spreads undivided, operates unspent.

(There is a couplet indeed.)

> Breathes in our soul, informs our mortal part,
> As full, as perfect, in a hair as heart;
> As full, as perfect, in vile man that mourns,
> As the rapt seraph that adores and burns:
> To Him no high, no low, no great, no small;
> He fills, He bounds, connects, and equals all."

Let me invite your attention to the few following lines on the apportionment of separate instincts or qualities to different animals, and be good enough to observe how the single words clench the whole argument. They are as descriptive as the bars of Haydn's music in the oratorio of the Creation:—

> "What modes of sight betwixt each wide extreme,
> The mole's dim curtain, and the lynx's beam;
> Of smell, the headlong lioness between,
> And hound sagacious on the tainted green;
> Of hearing, from the life that fills the flood,
> To that which warbles through the vernal wood.
> The spider's touch, how exquisitely fine!
> Feels at each thread, and lives along the line."

What a couplet again is that! It is only about a spider; but I guarantee its immortality.

If I set down the Terse, the Accurate, the Complete, the pungency of the Satiric point, the felicity of the well-turned Compliment, as the distinctive features of Pope's poetical excellence, it should not escape us that there are occasions when he reaches a high degree of moral energy and ardour. I have purposely excluded from our present consideration all scrutiny and dissection of Pope's real inner character. I am aware, that, taking it in the most favourable light, it can only be regarded as formed of mixed and imperfect elements; but I cannot refuse to myself the belief that when the Poet speaks in such strains as the following, they in some degree reflect and embody the spirit of the Man. I quote from his animated description of the triumph of vice:—

> "Let Greatness own her, and she's mean no more;
> Her birth, her beauty, crowds and courts confess,
> Chaste matrons praise her, and grave bishops bless;
> In golden chains the willing world she draws,
> And her's the Gospel is, and her's the laws;
> Mounts the tribunal, lifts her scarlet head,
> And sees pale virtue carted in her stead.
> Lo! at the wheels of her triumphal car,
> Old England's genius, rough with many a scar,
> Dragg'd in the dust! his arms hang idly round,
> His flag inverted trails along the ground!"

And, again with more special reference to himself,

> "Ask you what provocation I have had?
> The strong antipathy of good to bad.
> When truth or virtue an affront endures,
> Th' affront is mine, my friend, and should be yours.
> Yes, I am proud, I must be proud, to see
> Men not afraid of God, afraid of me:
> Safe from the bar, the pulpit, and the throne,
> Yet touch'd and sham'd by ridicule alone.
> O sacred weapon! left for truth's defence,
> Sole dread of folly, vice, and insolence!
> To all but heav'n-directed hands denied,
> The muse may give thee, but the gods must guide:
> Rev'rent I touch thee! but with honest zeal;
> To rouse the watchmen of the public weal,
> To virtue's work provoke the tardy Hall,
> And goad the prelate slumbering in his stall.
> Let envy howl, while heav'n's whole chorus sings,
> And bark at honour not conferr'd by kings;
> Let flatt'ry sickening see the incense rise,
> Sweet to the world, and grateful to the skies:
> Truth guards the poet, sanctifies the line,
> And makes immortal, verse as mean as mine."

My limits, more than my materials, warn me that I must desist. As, however, with reference to the single object which I have all along had in view, I think it more politic that I should let the words of Pope, rather than my own, leave the last echoes on your ear, I should like to conclude this address with his own concluding lines to perhaps the most important and highly-wrought of his poems, the "Essay on Man." They appear to me calculated to leave an appropriate impression of that orderly and graceful muse, whose attractions I have, feebly I know and inadequately, but with the honesty and warmth of a thorough sincerity, endeavoured to place before you; if I mistake not, you will trace in them, as in his works at large, the same perfect propriety of expression, the same refined simplicity of idea, the same chastened felicity of imagery, all animated and warmed by that feeling of devotion for Bolingbroke, which pervaded his poetry and his life:

> "Come then, my friend! my genius! come along;
> Oh master of the poet, and the song!

And while the muse now stoops, or now ascends
To man's low passions, or their glorious ends,
Teach me, like thee, in various nature wise,
To fall with dignity, with temper rise;
Form'd by thy converse, happily to steer
From grave to gay, from lively to severe;
Correct with spirit, eloquent with ease,
Intent to reason, or polite to please.
Oh! while along the stream of time thy name
Expanded flies, and gathers all its fame,
Say, shall my little bark attendant sail,
Pursue the triumph, and partake the gale?
When statesmen, heroes, kings, in dust repose,
Whose sons shall blush their fathers were thy foes,
Shall then this verse to future age pretend
Thou wert my guide, philosopher, and friend, —
That urg'd by thee, I turn'd the tuneful art
From sounds to things, from fancy to the heart;
For wit's false mirror held up nature's light;
Show'd erring pride, whatever is, is right;
That reason, passion, answer one great aim;
That true self-love and social are the same;
That virtue only makes our bliss below;
And all our knowledge is ourselves to know."

Gentlemen of the jury, that is my case.

LECTURE II.

TRAVELS IN AMERICA.

It may be known to some of those whom I have the pleasure to see around me, that when circumstances to which I need not further allude, occasioned a breach, temporary indeed, and soon repaired, in my connection with the West Riding of Yorkshire,—when, as the phrase goes, some of your neighbours, and probably of yourselves, had given me leave to go upon my travels,—I thought I could make no better use of this involuntary leisure than by acquiring some personal knowledge of the United States of America. I accordingly embarked in the autumn of the year 1841, and spent about one whole year in North America, having within that period passed nearly over the length and breadth of the Republic, trod at least the soil of twenty-two out of the twenty-six States of which the Union was then composed, and paid short visits to the Queen's dominions in Canada, and to the Island of Cuba. I determined to keep a journal during my travels, and only at the end of them to decide what should become of it when it was completed. I found it was written in too hurried and desultory a manner, and was too much confined to my own daily proceedings, to make it of interest to the public at large. Still more strongly I felt that, after having been received with uniform civility and attention, nay, I may say, with real warmth and openness of heart, I should not wish, even where I had nothing but what was most favourable to communicate, immediately to exhibit myself as an inquisitive observer of the interior life to which I had been admitted; and this very feeling would probably have disqualified me for the office of an impartial critic. Now, however, that above eight years have elapsed since my return, in turning over the pages then written, it has seemed to me allowable to endeavour, for a purpose like the present, to convey a few of the leading impressions which I derived from the surface of nature and society as they exhibited themselves in the New World.

It must follow necessarily from such limits as could be allowed to me on an occasion of this kind, that any account which I can put together from materials so vast and so crowded, must be the merest superficial skimming of the subject that can be conceived. All I can answer for is, that it shall be faithful to the feelings excited at the moment, and perfectly honest as far as it goes. I must premise one point with reference to what I have just now glanced at — the use of individual names. I came in contact with several of the public men, the historical men they will be, of the American Republic. I shall think myself at liberty occasionally to depart in their instance from the rule of strict abstinence which I have otherwise prescribed to myself, and to treat them as public property, so long as I say nothing to their disadvantage. On the other hand, the public men of the United States are not created faultless beings, any more than the public men of other countries; it must not, therefore, be considered when I mention with pleasure anything which redounds to their credit, that I am intending to present you with their full and complete portraits.

It was on the 21st day of October, upon a bright crisp morning, that the *Columbia* steam-packet, upon which I was a passenger, turned the lighthouse outside the harbour of Boston. The whole effect of the scene was cheerful and pleasing; the bay is studded with small islands, bare of trees, but generally crowned with some sparkling white building, frequently some public establishment. The town rises well from the water, and the shipping and the docks wore the look of prosperous commerce. As I stood by some American friends acquired during the voyage, and heard them point out the familiar villages, and villas, and institutions, with patriotic pleasure, I could not altogether repress some slight but not grudging envy of those who were to bring so long a voyage to an end in their own country, amidst their own family, within their own homes. I am not aware I ever again experienced, during my whole American sojourn, the peculiar feeling of the stranger. It was, indeed, dispelled at the moment, when their flag ship, the *Columbus*, gave our *Columbia* a distinguished, and, I thought, touching reception; the crew manned the yards, cheered, and then the band played, first, "God Save the Queen," and then "Yankee Doodle." I spent altogether, at two different intervals, about a month in Boston.

I look back with fond recollection to its well-built streets — the swelling dome of its State-house — the pleasant walks on what is termed the Common — a park, in fact, of moderate size, in the centre of the city, where I made my first acquaintance with the bright winter sunsets of America, and the peculiar transparent green and opal tints which stripe the skies around them — the long wooden causeways across the inner harbour, which rather recalled St. Petersburgh to my recollection — the newly-erected granite obelisk on a neighbouring height, which certainly had no affinity with St. Petersburgh, as it was to mark the spot, sacred to an American, of the battle of Bunker's Hill — the old elm tree, at the suburban university of Cambridge, beneath which Washington drew his sword in order to take the command of the national army — the shaded walks and glades of Mount Auburn, the beautiful cemetery of Boston, to which none that we yet have can be compared, but which I trust before long our Chadwicks and Paxtons may enable us to imitate, and perhaps to excel. These are some of my external recollections of Boston; but there are some fonder still, of the most refined and animated social intercourse — of hospitalities which it seemed impossible to exhaust — of friendships which I trust can never be effaced. Boston appears to me, certainly, on the whole, the American town in which an Englishman of cultivated and literary tastes, or of philanthropic pursuits, would feel himself most at home. The residence here was rendered peculiarly agreeable to me by a friendship with one of its inhabitants, which I had previously made in England; he hardly yet comes within my rule of exception, but I do not give up the notion of his becoming one of the historical men of his country. However, it is quite open for me to mention some of those with whom, mainly through his introduction, I here became acquainted. There was Mr. Justice Story, whose reputation and authority as a commentator and expounder of law stand high wherever law is known or honoured, and who was, what at least is more generally attractive, one of the most generous and single-hearted of men. He was an enthusiastic admirer of this country, especially of its lawyers; how he would kindle up and flow on if he touched upon Lord Hardwick or Lord Mansfield — "Sir," as an American always begins, "on the prairies of Illinois, this day Lord Mansfield administers the law of commerce." He had also a very exalted opinion of the judgments of Lord Stowell, which his own studies and practice had lead him thoroughly to appreciate; and I may permit myself to say that he had formed a high estimate of the judicial powers of Lord Cottenham.

I must admit one thing—when he was in the room few others could get in a word; but it was impossible to resent this, for he talked evidently not to bear down others, but because he could not help it. Then there was Dr. Channing. I could not hear him preach, as his physical powers were nearly exhausted; but on one or two occasions I was admitted to his house. You found a fragile frame, and a dry manner, but you soon felt that you were in a presence in which nothing that was impure, base, or selfish, could breathe at ease. There was the painter, Alston, a man of real genius, who suffices to prove that the domain of the fine arts, though certainly not hitherto the most congenial to the American soil, may be successfully brought, to use their current phrase, into annexation with it. These, alas! have, since my visit, all been taken away. In the more immediate department of letters there are happily several who yet remain—Mr. Bancroft, the able and accomplished historian of his own country — Mr. Ticknor, who has displayed the resources of a well-stored and accomplished mind in his recent work on the literature of Spain — Mr. Longfellow, with whose feeling and graceful poetry many must be acquainted—Mr. Emerson, who has been heard and admired in this country—and I crown my list with Mr. Prescott, the historian of Ferdinand and Isabella, of Mexico, and of Peru, with respect to whom, during the visit he paid to England in the past summer, I had the satisfaction of witnessing how all that was most eminent in this country confirmed the high estimate I had myself formed of his head, and the higher one of his heart.

The public institutions of Boston are admirably conducted. The Public or Common Schools there, as I believe in New England generally, are supported by a general rate, to which all contribute, and all may profit by. I am not naturally now disposed to discuss the question, how far this system would bear being transplanted and engrafted on our polity; but it would be uncandid if I did not state that the universality of the instruction, and the excellence of what fell under my own observation, presented to my mind some mortifying points of contrast with what we have hitherto effected at home. It is well known that a large proportion of the more wealthy and cultivated part of the society of Boston belong to the Unitarian persuasion; but a considerable number of the middle classes, and especially of the rural population of New England, comprising the six Northern States of the Union, still retain much of the Puritan tenets and habits of their immediate ancestors,—their Pilgrim Fathers.

Before I leave Boston, let me add one observation on a lighter topic. I lodged at the Tremont Hotel, which was admirably conducted, like very many of those imposing establishments in the chief cities of the Union. Here I learnt that one is apt to receive false impressions at first; I was struck with the clean, orderly, agile appearance of the waiters. "The Americans beat us hollow in waiters," was my inner thought; on inquiring I found that of the twenty-five waiters in the house, four were English and twenty-one Irish. I could not help wishing that a large number of the Irish might come and be waiters for a little while.

Within three or four days of my landing I grew impatient to see the falls of Niagara, without loss of time; if any sudden event should have summoned me home, I felt how much I should have grudged crossing the Atlantic without having been at Niagara; and I also wished to look upon the autumn tints of the American forests, before the leaves, already beginning to fall, had entirely disappeared. The Western Railway, which appeared to me the best constructed that I saw in America, took me to Albany, a distance of 200 miles. The railway carriages, always there called cars, consist of long rooms, rather like a dining-room of a steam-packet, with a stove inside, often a most desirable addition in the American winter; and you can change your seat or walk about as you choose. They are generally rougher than our railways, and the whole getting-up of the line is of a ruder and cheaper character; they do not impede the view as much as with us, as they make no scruple of dashing across or alongside of the main street in the towns or villages through which they pass. But I ought to remark about this as about every thing else, that the work of progress and transformation goes on with such enormous rapidity, that the interval of eight years since my visit will probably have made a large portion of my remarks thoroughly obsolete.

The New England country through which we passed looks cheerful, interspersed with frequent villages and numerous churches, bearing the mark at the same time of the long winter and barren soil with which the stout Puritan blood of Britain has so successfully contended; indeed, the only staple productions of a district which supplies seamen for all the Union, and ships over all the world, are said to be ice and granite.

Albany is the capital of the state of New York, — the Empire State, as its inhabitants love to call it, and it is a name which it deserves, as fairly as our own old Yorkshire would deserve to be called the Empire County of England. It is rather an imposing town, rising straight above the Hudson river, gay with some gilded domes, and many white marble columns, only they are too frequently appended to houses of very staring red brick. From Albany to Utica, the railroad follows the stream of the Mohawk, which recalls the name of the early Indian dwellers in that bright valley, still retaining its swelling outline of wood-covered hills, but gay with prosperous villages and busy cultivation. I was perhaps still more struck the next evening, though it was a more level country, where the railway passes in the midst of the uncleared or clearing forest, and suddenly bursts out of a pine glade or cedar swamp into the heart of some town, probably four, three, or two years old, with tall white houses, well-lighted shops, billiard-rooms, &c.; and emerging, as we did, from the dark shadows into the full moonlight, the wooden spires, domes, and porticoes of the infant cities looked every bit as if they had been hewn out of the marble quarries of Carrara. I am aware that it is not the received opinion; but there is something both in the outward aspect of this region and the general state of society accompanying it, which to me seemed eminently poetical. What can be more striking or stirring, despite the occasional rudeness of the forms, than all this enterprise, energy, and life welling up in the desert? At the towns of Syracuse, of Auburn, and of Rochester, I experienced the sort of feeling which takes away one's breath; the process seemed actually going on before one's eyes, and one hardly knows whether to think it as grand as the Iliad, or as quaint as a harlequin farce. I will quote the words I wrote down at the time: —

"The moment is not come for me yet, if it ever should come, to make me feel myself warranted in forming speculations upon far results, upon guarantees for future endurance and stability; all that I can now do is to look and to marvel at what is before my eyes. I do not think I am deficient in relish for antiquity and association: I know that I am English, not in a pig-headed adhesion to everything there, but in heart to its last throb. Yet I cannot be unmoved or callous to the soarings of Young America, in such legitimate and laudable directions too; and I feel that it is already not the least bright, and may be the most enduring, title of my country to the homage of mankind, that she has produced such a people. May God employ them both for his own high glory!"

I am bound here in candour to state that I think what I first saw in America was, with little exception, the best of its kind; such was the society of Boston — such was the energy of progress in the western portion of the State of New York.

At Rochester, an odd coincidence occurred to me, striking enough I think to be mentioned, though it only concerned myself. After the arrival of the railway carriage, and the usual copious meal of tea and meat that ensues, I had been walking about the town, which dates only from 1812, and then contained 20,000 inhabitants, and as I was returning to the hotel, I saw the word Theatre written up. Wishing to see everything in a new country, I climbed up some steep stairs into what was little better than a garret, where I found a rude theatre, and ruder audience, consisting chiefly of boys, who took delight in pelting one another. There was something, however, at which I had a right to feel surprised. In a playhouse of strollers, at a town nearly five hundred miles in the interior of America, which, thirty years before, had no existence, thus coming in by the merest chance, I saw upon the drop-scene the most accurate representation of my own house, Naworth Castle, in Cumberland.

A great improvement has recently occurred in the nomenclature of this district; formerly a too classical surveyor of the State of New York had christened — I used the wrong term, had heathenised, to make a new one, — all the young towns and villages by the singularly inapplicable titles of Utica, Ithaca, Palmyra, Rome: they are now reverting to the far more appropriate, and, I should say, more harmonious Indian names, indigenous to the soil, such as Oneida, Onondaga, Cayuga.

I thought my arrival at Niagara very interesting. We had come to Lockport, where there is a chain of magnificent locks, on the Erie Canal, one of the great public works of America, and which has done much to enrich this Empire State of New York. The surplus of the receipts has enabled it to execute a variety of other public works. We arrived too late for the usual public conveyance. The proprietor of the stage-coach agreed to give me, with one or two other Englishmen, a lumber waggon to convey us to the falls. The Colonel, for he was one, as I found the drivers of the coaches often were, drove his team of four horses himself. I generally found the stage-coach driving in the United States indescribably rough, but the drivers very adroit in their steerage, and always calling their horses by their names, and addressing them as reasonable beings, to which they seemed quite to respond. Altogether, the strangeness of the vehicle, the cloudless beauty of the night, the moonlight streaming through the forest glades, the meeting a party of the Tuscarora Indians, who still have a settlement here, the first hearing the noise of Niagara about seven miles off, and the growing excitement of the nearer approach, gave to the whole drive a most stirring and enjoyable character. When I arrived at the hotel, the Cataract House, I would not anticipate by any moonlight glimpses the full disclosures of the coming day, but reserved my first visit for the clear light and freshened feelings of the morning.

I staid five days at Niagara on that occasion; I visited it again twice, having travelled several thousands of miles in each interval. I have thus looked upon it in the late autumn, in the early spring, and in the full summer. Mrs. Butler, in her charming work on America, when she comes to Niagara, says only, " Who can describe that sight? " and, with these words, finishes her book. There is not merely the difficulty of finding adequate words, but there is a simplicity and absence, as I should say, of incidents in the scenery, or, at least, so entire a subordination of them to the main great spectacle, that attempts at description would seem inapplicable as well as impotent. Nevertheless, I have undertaken, however inadequately, the attempt to place before you the impressions which I actually derived from the most prominent objects that I saw in America. How, then, can I wholly omit Niagara? The first view neither in the least disappointed, or surprised, but it wholly satisfied me. I felt it to be complete, and that nothing could go beyond it: volume, majesty, might, are the first ideas which it conveys: on nearer and more familiar inspection, I appreciated other attributes and beauties — the emerald crest — the seas of spray — the rainbow wreaths. Pictures and panoramas had given me a correct apprehension of the form and outline; but they fail, for the same reason as language would, to impart an idea of the whole effect, which is not picturesque, though it is sublime; there is also the technical drawback in painting of the continuous mass of white, and the line of the summit of the Fall is as smooth and even as a common mill-dam. Do not imagine, however, that the effect could be improved by being more picturesque; just as there are several trivial and unsightly buildings on the banks, but Niagara can be no more spoiled than it can be improved. You would, when on the spot, no more think of complaining that Niagara was not picturesque, than you would remark in the shock and clang of battle that a trumpet sounded out of tune. Living at Niagara was not like ordinary life; its not over loud but constant solemn roar has in itself a mysterious sound: is not the highest voice to which the Universe can ever listen compared by inspiration to the sound of many waters? The whole of existence there has a dreamy but not a frivolous impress; you feel that you are not in the common world, but in its sublimest temple.

I naturally left such a place and such a life with keen regret, but I was already the last visitor of the year, and the hotels were about to close. I was told that I had already been too late for the best tints of autumn (or fall, as the Americans picturesquely term that season), and that they were at no time so vivid that year as was usual; I saw, however, great richness and variety of hue; I think the bright soft yellow of the sugar maple, and the dun red of the black oak, were the most remarkable. These and the beech, the white cedar, the hemlock spruce, the hickory, with occasionally the chesnut and walnut, seemed the prevailing trees in all this district. I can well imagine a person being disappointed in the American Forest; trees, such as those at Wentworth and Castle Howard (may I say?) seem the exception, and not the rule. The mass of them run entirely to height, and are too thick together, and there is a great deal too much dead fir; still there is a great charm and freshness in the American forest, derived partly perhaps from association, when you look through the thick tracery of its virgin glades.

On my going back I paid two visits at country houses; one to an old gentleman, Mr. Wadsworth, most distinguished in appearance, manner, and understanding, who had settled where I found him, fifty years before, when he had not a white neighbour within thirty miles, or a flour mill within fifty; he lived entirely surrounded by Indians, who have now disappeared. On some occasion, there had been a review of a corps of militia. A neighbouring Indian Chief had been present, and was observed to be very dejected; Mr. Wadsworth went up to him, and offered refreshment, which was usually very acceptable, but he declined it. Upon being pressed to say what was the matter, he answered with a deep sigh, pointing to the east, "You are the rising sun"—then to the west, "We are the setting." The face of the country is now, indeed, changed; a small flourishing town, the capital of the county, stretches from the gate; and the house overlooks one of the richest and best cultivated tracts in America, the valley of the Gennessee. I fancy that quotations of the price of Gennessee wheat are familiar to the frequenters of our corn markets. My host was one of the comparatively few persons in the United States who have tenants under them holding farms; among them I found three Yorkshiremen from my own neighbourhood, one of whom showed me what he called the *gainest* way to the house, which I recognised as a genuine Yorkshire term; he told me that his landlord was the first nobleman in the country, which is also clearly not an Americanism. While on this topic I may mention that, on another occasion, I was taken to drink tea at a farmer's house in New England. We had been regaled most hospitably, when the farmer took the friend who had brought me aside, and asked what part of England Lord Morpeth came from? "From Yorkshire, I believe," said my friend. "Well, I should not have thought that from his manner of talking," was the reply.

My other visit was to Mr. Van Buren, who had been the last President of the United States, and who, I suspect, shrewdly reckoned on being the next. It seemed, indeed, at that time to be the general expectation among his own, the Democratic, or, as they were then commonly called, the Loco-foco party. He was at that time living on his farm of Kinderhook; the house was modest and extremely well ordered, and nothing could exceed the courtesy or fullness of his conversation. He abounded in anecdotes of all the public men of his country. In his dining-room were pictures of Jefferson and General Jackson, the great objects of his political devotion. On my return through Albany, I had an interview with Mr. Seward, then for the second time Governor of the State of New York. I find that I noted at the time, that he was the first person I had met who did not speak slightingly of the Abolitionists; he thought they were gradually gaining ground. He had already acted a spirited part on points connected with slavery, especially in a contest with the legislature of Virginia concerning the delivery of fugitive slaves.

I approached the city of New York by the Hudson. The whole course of that river from Albany, as seen from the decks of the countless steamers that ply along it, is singularly beautiful, especially where it forces a passage through the barriers of the Highlands, which, however, afford no features of rugged grandeur like our friends in Scotland; but though the forms are steep and well-defined, their rich green outlines of waving wood, inclosing, in smooth many-curved reaches, the sail-covered bosom of the stately river, present nothing but soft and smiling images. I then took up my winter quarters at New York. I thought this, the commercial and fashionable, though not the political, capital of the Union, a very brilliant city. To give the best idea of it, I should describe it as something of a fusion between Liverpool and Paris — crowded quays, long perspectives of vessels and masts, bustling streets, gay shops, tall white houses, and a clear brilliant sky overhead. There is an absence of solidity in the general appearance, but in some of the new buildings they are successfully availing themselves of their ample resources in white marble and granite. At the point of the Battery, where the long thoroughfare of Broadway, extending some miles, pushes its green fringe into the wide harbour, with its glancing waters and graceful shipping, and the limber, long raking masts, which look so different from our own, and the soft swelling outline of the receding shores, New York has a special character and beauty of its own. I spent about a month here very pleasantly; the society appeared to me on the whole to have a less solid and really refined character than that of Boston, but there is more of animation, gaiety, and sparkle in the daily life. In point of hospitality, neither could outdo the other.

Keeping to my rule of only mentioning names which already belong to fame, I may thus distinguish the late Chancellor Kent, whose commentaries are well known to professional readers: he had been obliged, by what I think the very unwise law of the State of New York, to retire from his high legal office at the premature age of sixty, and there I found him at seventy-eight, full of animation and racy vigour, which, combined with great simplicity, made his conversation most agreeable.—Washington Irving, a well-known name both to American and English ears, whose nature appears as gentle and genial as his works—I cannot well give higher praise:

— Mr. Bryant, in high repute as a poet, and others. I had the pleasure of making acquaintance with many of the families of those who had been the foremost men in their country, Hamiltons, Jays, Livingstones. I lodged at the Astor House, a large hotel conducted upon a splendid scale; and I cannot refrain from one, I fear rather sensual, allusion to the oyster cellars of New York; in no part of the world have I ever seen places of refreshment as attractive — every one seems to eat oysters all day long. What signifies more, the public institutions and schools are extremely well conducted. The churches of the different denominations are very numerous and well filled. It is my wish to touch very lightly upon any point which among us, among even some of us now here, may be matter of controversy; I, however, honestly think that the experience of the United States does not as yet enable them to decide on either side the argument between the Established and Voluntary systems in religion: take the towns by themselves, and I think the voluntary principle appears fully adequate to satisfy all religious exigencies; then it must be remembered that the class which makes the main difficulty elsewhere, scarcely if at all exists in America; it is the blessed privilege of the United States, and it is one which goes very far to counterbalance any drawbacks at which I may have to hint, that they really have not, as a class, any poor among them. A real beggar is what you never see. On the other hand, over their immense tracts of territory, the voluntary system has not sufficed to produce sufficient religious accommodation; it may, however, be truly questioned, whether any establishment would be equal to that function. This is, however, one among the many questions which the republican experience of America has not yet solved. As matters stand at present, indifference to religion cannot be fairly laid to her charge; probably religious extremes are pushed farther than elsewhere; there certainly is a breadth and universality of religious liberty which I do not regard without some degree of envy.

Upon my progress southward, I made a comparatively short halt at Philadelphia. This fair city has not the animation of New York, but it is eminently well built, neat, and clean beyond parallel. The streets are all at right angles with each other, and bear the names of the different trees of the country; the houses are of red brick, and mostly have white marble steps and silver knockers, all looking bright and shining under the effect of copious and perpetual washing. It still looks like a town constructed by Quakers, who were its original founders; but by Quakers who had become rather dandified. .The waterworks established here are deservedly celebrated; each house can have as much water as it likes, within and without, at every moment, for about 18s. a year. I hope our towns will be emulous of this great advantage. I think it right to say that in our general arrangements for health and cleanliness we appear to me very much to excel the Americans, and our people look infinitely healthier, stouter, rosier, jollier; the greater proportion of Americans with whom you converse would be apt to tell you they were dyspeptic, whether principally from the dry quality of their atmosphere, the comparatively little exercise which they take, or the rapidity with which they accomplish their meals, I will not take upon myself to pronounce. There is one point of advantage which they turn to account, especially in all their new towns, which is, that their immense command of space enables them to isolate almost every house, and thus secure an ambient atmosphere for ventilation. In my first walk through Philadelphia I passed the glittering white marble portico of the United States Bank, which, after the recent crash it had sustained, made me think of whited sepulchres. Near it was a pile, with a respectable old English appearance, of far nobler association; this was the State House, where the Declaration of American Independence was signed, — one of the most pregnant acts of which history bears record. It contains a picture of William Penn and a statue of Washington. While I was there, a sailor from the State of Maine, with a very frank and jaunty air, burst into the room, and in a glow of ardent patriotism inquired, "Is this the room in which the Declaration of Independence was signed?" When he found that I was an Englishman, he seemed, with real good breeding, to be afraid that he had grated on my feelings, and told me that in the year 1814 our flag had waved over the two greatest capitals of the world, Washington and Paris. I looked with much interest at the great Model Prison of the separate system. I was favourably impressed with all that met the eye, but I refrain from entering upon the vexed question of comparison between this and the silent and other systems, as I feel how much the solution must depend upon ever recurring experience. The poor-house, like that at New York, is built and administered on a very costly scale, and also has a great proportion of foreigners as inmates, and of the foreigners a great proportion Irish. This seems to enhance the munificence of the provision for destitution; at the same time, it is not to be forgotten that the foreign labour is an article of nearly essential necessity to the progress of the country. On the only Sunday which I sent in Philadelphia, I went to a church which was not wanting in associations; the communion plate had been given by Queen Anne, and I sat in the pew of General Washington. I was told by some one that his distinguished cotemporary, Chief Justice Marshall, said of him, that, in contradiction to what was often thought, he was a man of decided genius, but he was such a personification of wisdom, that he never put anything forward which the occasion did not absolutely require. It seemed to me that there was at Philadelphia a greater separation and exclusiveness in society, more resemblance to what would be called a fashionable class in European cities, than I had found in America elsewhere.

My next brief pause was at Baltimore. At a halt on the railroad on the way thither, I heard a conductor or guard say to a negro, " I cannot let you go, for you are a SLAVE." This was my first intimation that I had crossed the border which divides Freedom from Slavery. I quote from the entry which I made upon noting these words that evening: — " Declaration of Independence which I read yesterday — pillar of Washington which I have looked on to-day — what are ye?"

I must now give myself some little vent. It was a subject which I felt during my whole sojourn in America, as I feel it still, to be paramount in interest to every other. It was one on which I intended and endeavoured to observe a sound discretion; we have not ourselves long enough washed off the stain to give us the right to rail at those whom we had originally inoculated with the pest; and a stranger abundantly experiencing hospitality could not with any propriety interfere wantonly upon the most delicate and difficult point of another nation's policy. I could not, however, fail often and deeply to feel, in the progress of my intercourse with many in that country — " Come not, my soul, into their secret; to their counsel, my honour, be not thou united." At the same time, I wished never to make any compromise of my opinion. I made it a point to pay special respect to the leading Abolitionists — those who had laboured or suffered in the cause — when I came within reach of them; at Boston, I committed the more overt act of attending the annual anti-slavery fair, by which I believe some thought I unduly committed myself. I was much struck in the distinguished and agreeable companies which I had the good fortune to frequent, with a few honourable exceptions, at the tone of disparagement, contempt, and anger, with which the Abolitionists were mentioned; just as any patrician company, in this country, would talk of a Socialist, or a Red Republican. I am, of course, now speaking of the free Northern States; in the South an Abolitionist could not be known to exist. My impression is, that in the interval since my visit, the dislike, the anger, has remained, and may, probably, have been heightened, but that the feeling of slight, of ignoring (to use a current phrase) their very existence, must have been sensibly checked. There were some who told me that they made it the business of their lives to superintend the passage of the runaway slaves through the free States; they reckoned, at that time, that about one thousand yearly escaped into Canada. I doubt whether the enactment and operation of the Fugitive Slave Bill will damp the ardour of their exertions. It may be easy to speak discreetly and plausibly about the paramount duty of not contravening the law; but how would you feel, my countrymen, if a fugitive was at your feet and the man-hunter at the door? I admit that the majesty of the law is on one side; but the long, deep misery of a whole human life is on the other. What you ought to feel is fervent gratitude to the Power which has averted from your shores and hearths this fearful trial, and, let me add, a heartfelt sympathy with those who are sustaining it.

At Baltimore I thought there was a more picturesque disposition of ground than in any other city of the Union: it is built on swelling eminences, commanding views of the widening Chesapeake, a noble arm of the sea. There are an unusual number of public monuments for an American town, and hence it has been christened the Monumental City. I found the same hospitality which had greeted me everywhere, and the good living seemed to me carried to its greatest height; they have in perfection the terrapin, a kind of land tortoise, and the canvass-back duck, a most unrivalled bird in any country. With reference to the topic I have lately touched upon, a Slave-holders' Convention was being held at the time of my visit for the State of Maryland. They had been led to adopt this step by their apprehensions both of the increase of the free coloured population, and what they termed their demoralising action on the slaves. The language, as reported, did not seem to have been very violent, but they very nearly subjected to lynch-law a man whom they suspected to be a reporter for an abolitionist newspaper. I dined with the daughter of Charles Carroll, who, when signing the Declaration of Independence, was told by a bystander that he would incur no danger, as there were so many of the same name — " of Carrollton," he added to his name, and I think it is the only one upon the document which has any appendage. Being thus nobly fathered, it is rather curious that this venerable lady should have been the mother of three English peeresses. The Roman Catholic Archbishop of Baltimore was one of the company; the assumption of that title does not appear in any degree to discompose the serenity of the Great Republic.

From Baltimore I transferred myself to Washington, the seat of government and capital of the American Union. I never saw so strange a place; it affords the strongest contrast to the regularity, compactness, neatness, and animation of the Atlantic cities I had hitherto visited. It is spread over a very large space, in this way justifying the expression of some one who wished to pay it a compliment, but did not know very well what attribute to select, so he termed it a " city of magnificent distances," over which it extends, or rather sprawls; it looks as if it had rained houses at random, or like half a dozen indifferent villages scattered over a goose common. Here and there, as if to heighten the contrast with the meanness of the rest, there are some very handsome public buildings; and the American Capitol, the meeting-place of the legislature and the seat of empire, though not exempt from architectural defects, towers proudly on a steep ascent, commanding the subject town and the course of the broad Potomac, which makes the only redeeming feature of the natural landscape. In short, while almost every other place which I saw in America gives the impression of life and progress, Washington not only appears stagnant, but retrograde. No busy commerce circulates in its streets; no brilliant shops diversify its mean ranges of ill-built houses; but very few equipages move along its wide, splashy, dreary avenues. I saw it, too, in the prime of its season, during the sitting of Congress. When it is not sitting, the members of the legislature and officers of the government dispose themselves over the breadth of the Union, and leave the capital to the clerks of the public offices, and

— does it not seem profanation to say it? — the *Slaves*, who are still permitted to inhabit what should rightly be the Metropolis of Freedom. It is at least gratifying to know that, in the last session of Congress, the slave-trade has been abolished in the district of Columbia, the small portion of territory immediately annexed to Washington. When they are here, the members of Congress are mostly packed together in large and very inferior boarding-houses, a great portion of them not bringing their wives and families over the immense distances they have to traverse; hence it also happens that Washington will appear to the stranger not merely one of the least thriving but also the least hospitable of American cities. I spent nearly a month there, and it was the only place in which I (what is termed) kept house, that is, I resided in private lodgings, and found my own food, a method of life, however, which, in the long run, has more comfort and independence than that of the huge hotels. It was a contrast, however, to the large armies of waiters to which I had grown accustomed, to have no one in the house but an old woman and a negro boy, the first of whom my English servant characterised as cross, and the second as stupid. I believe it was the policy of the founders of the Republic to place the seat of government where it would not be liable to be distracted by the turmoil of commerce, or over-awed by the violence of mobs; we have heard very lately of speculations to remove the seat of the French Government from Paris. Another cause which has probably contributed to check any designs for the external improvement and development of Washington, must have been the doubt how far in a nation which is extending its boundaries westward at so prodigious a rate, it will be desirable or possible long to retain as the seat of government a spot which will have become so little central.

What gave most interest to my stay at Washington naturally was the opportunity of attending the sittings of Congress. The interior of the Capitol is imposing, as well as the exterior; in the centre hall there were five large pictures, illustrating the prominent points of American history, which must be more agreeable to American than to British eyes. There is also a fine colossal statue of Washington, who is universally and not unduly called the father of his country. The chamber where the Senate meets is handsome and convenient. The general aspect of the assembly, which (as is well known) shares largely both in the legislative and executive powers of the constitution, is grave and decorous. The House of Representatives, the more popular branch of the government, returned by universal suffrage, assemble in a chamber of very imposing appearance, arranged rather as a theatre, in shape like the arc of a bow, but it is the worst room for hearing I ever was in : we hear of complaints occasionally of our Houses of Parliament, old and new, but they are faultless in comparison. In parts of the House it is impossible to hear any body, in others it answers all the purposes of a whispering gallery, and I have heard members carry on a continuous dialogue while a debate was storming around them. Both in the Senate and the House every member has a most commodious arm-chair, a desk for his papers, and a spitting-box, to which he does not always confine himself. I came very often, and it was impossible to surpass the attention I received; some member's seat in the body of the House was always given to me, and I was at liberty to remain there during the whole of the debate, listen to what was going on, or write my letters, as I chose. The palpable distinction between them and our House of Commons I should say to be this, we are more noisy, and they are more disorderly. They do not cheer, they do not cough, but constantly several are speaking at a time, and they evince a contemptuous disregard for the decisions of their Speaker. They have no recognized leaders of the different parties, the members of Government not being allowed to have seats in either House of Congress, and the respective parties do not occupy distinct quarters in the Chamber, so that you may often hear a furious wrangle being carried on between two nearly contiguous members. While I was at Washington, the question of slavery, or at least of points connected with slavery, gave the chief colour and animation to the discussions in the House of Representatives. Old Mr. Adams, the ex-president of the United States, occupied, without doubt, the most prominent position; he presented a very striking appearance, standing up erect at the age of 73, having once filled the highest post attainable by an American citizen, with trembling hands and eager eyes, in defence of the right of petition, — the right to petition against the continuance of slavery in the district of Columbia—with a majority of the House usually deciding against him, and a portion of it lashed into noise and storm. I thought it was very near being, and to some extent it was, quite a sublime position, but it rather detracted from the grandeur of the effect at least, that his own excitement was so great as to pitch his voice almost into a screech, and to make him more disorderly than all the rest. He put one in mind of a fine old game-cock, and occasionally showed great energy and power of sarcasm. I had certainly an opportunity of forming my opinion, as I sat through a speech of his that lasted three days; but then it is fair to mention that the actual sittings hardly last above three hours a day — about four dinner is ready, and they go away for the day, differing much herein from our practice; and on this occasion they frequently allowed Mr. Adams to sit down to rest. All the time I believe he was not himself for the discontinuance of slavery, even in the district of Columbia, but he contended that the constitution had accorded the free right of petition.* One morning he presented a petition for the dissolution of the Union, which raised a great tempest. Mr. Marshall, of Kentucky, a fine and graceful speaker, moved a vote of censure upon him. Another member, whom I need not name, the ablest and fiercest champion whom I heard on the southern or slave-holder side, made a most savage onslaught on Mr. Adams; then up got that " old man eloquent," and no one could have reproached him with not understanding how to speak even daggers. His brave but somewhat troublous spirit has passed from the scenes upon which he played so conspicuous a part, but he has left behind him some words of fire, the 'sparks of which are not yet extinct. Nothing came of all this stir; I used to meet Mr. Adams at dinner while it went on, very calm and undisturbed. After seeing and hearing what takes place in some of these sittings, one is tempted to think that the Union must break up next morning; but the flame appeared generally to smoulder almost as quickly as it ignited. The debates in the Senate, during the same period, were dignified, business-like, and not very lively; so it may be judged which House had most attraction for the passing traveller. I heard Mr. Clay in the Senate once, but every one told me that he was labouring under feebleness and exhaustion, so that I could only perceive the great charm in the tones of his voice. I think this most attractive quality was still more perceivable in private intercourse, and I certainly never met any public man, either in his country or in mine, always excepting Mr. Canning, who exercised such

---

* I have lately met with a curious proof that this very eminent man was not exempt from the usual susceptibility of his countrymen on the subject of colour. In a letter to the accomplished American actor, Mr. Hackett, he says, that the moral of the tragedy of Othello is to show how improper it is to mix white blood with black.

evident fascination over the minds and affections of his friends and followers, as Henry Clay. I thought his society most attractive, easy, simple, and genial, with great natural dignity. If his countrymen made better men presidents, I should applaud their virtue in resisting the spell of his eloquence and attractions; when the actual list is considered, my respect for the discernment elicited by universal suffrage does not stand at a very high point. Another great man, Daniel Webster, I could not hear in either House of Congress, because he then filled, as he does now, the high office of Secretary of State; but it is quite enough to look on his jutting dark brow, and cavernous eyes, and massive forehead, to be assured that they are the abode of as much, if not more, intellectual power than any head you perhaps ever remarked. For many, if not for all reasons, I am well content that he should be again at the head of the American Cabinet, for I feel sure that while he is even intensely American, he has an enlightened love of peace, and a cordial sympathy with the fortunes and glories of the old, as well as the new, Anglo-Saxon stock. The late Mr. Calhoun, who impressed most of those who were thrown in his way with a high opinion of his ability, his honesty, and, I may add, his impracticability, I had not the good fortune to hear in public, or meet in private society. It is well known that his attachment to the maintenance of slavery went so far as to lead him to declare that real freedom could not be maintained without it. Among those who at that time contributed both to the credit and gaiety of the society of Washington, I cannot forbear adding the name of Mr. Legare, then the Attorney-general of the Union, now unhappily, like too many of those whom I have had occasion to mention, no longer living. He appeared to me the best scholar, and the most generally accomplished man, I met in all the Union. I may feel biassed in his favour, for I find among my entries, "Mr. Legare spoke tonight of Pope as he ought."

I have not mentioned what might be thought of a very prominent object at Washington — the President of the United States. He resides for his term of office at a substantial plain building, called the White House. Mr. Tyler filled the office when I was there, and appeared a simple, unaffected person. Washington is the head quarters of another branch of the Constitution, which works perhaps with less of friction and censure than any other — the Supreme Court of Judicature. The large federal questions between State and State give great weight and interest to its proceedings. I heard an interesting cause between the States of Maryland and Pennsylvania; it was an action to try the constitutional validity of an Act of the State of Pennsylvania, which gave a trial by jury to the fugitive slave. How this subject pursued and pervaded every thing! It was argued with great ability on both sides; it was ultimately ruled against the power of the free states to pass such an act; and the recent Fugitive Slave Law may probably have arisen out of some such debateable questions of right; at all events, it has entirely swept away the intervention of a jury.

The last day of my abode at Washington was spent becomingly at Mount Vernon, the residence, and now the grave, of Washington. It is well placed on a wooded hill above the noble Potomac, here a mile and a half broad. The tomb is a sad affair for such a man; it has an inscription upon it denoting that it was erected by John Strutters, marble mason! It is placed under a glaring red building, something between a coach-house and a cage. The Senate once procured the consent of the family to have it removed to the Capitol, when a bricklayer, a labourer, and a cart arrived to take it off one morning, at which their indignation naturally rose. There are few things remarkable in the house, except the key of the Bastille sent by General Lafayette to General Washington, and a sword given to him by Frederick the Great, with this address, "From the Oldest General of the age to the Best." I was gratified to see a print from my picture of the Three Maries. I wonder if it ever excited the interest and the piety of Washington?

I made a rapid journey, by steamboat and railroad, through the States of Virginia and North Carolina; the country wore a universal impress of exhaustion, desertion, slavery. It appears to be one of the trials for the cupidity of man, that slavery, notwithstanding all its drawbacks, has a certain degree of adaptation, not, I trust, in the mercy of God, a necessary adaptation, to the culture of fertile soils in hot climates; but in sterile or exhausted soils, where the energy of man must be called out to overcome difficulties, it is evident that slavery has no elastic spring or restorative power.

Richmond, the capital of Virginia, has a certain resemblance in position to its namesake in Surrey. I saw the local legislature in session; it was very full of coarse-looking farmers from the western portion of the state: it struck me that the acute town lawyers must manage matters much as they choose. I never saw a country so hopeless as all that I passed through in North Carolina — a flat, sandy waste of pines, with scarcely a habitation. I spent a fortnight at Charleston, the capital of her more energetic sister, South Carolina. This town and state may be looked upon as the head-quarters of the slave-holding interest; and repeatedly, when they have thought the policy of the North too encroaching, either upon questions relating to what they term their peculiar institutions, which is their euphonious description of slavery, or, when we should feel a juster sympathy with them, upon questions relating to the protection of the northern manufactures in opposition to a liberal commercial policy, they have not only held the very highest tone in favour of a dissolution of the Union, but have proceeded to overt acts of resistance. I am bound to say that I spent my time there very pleasantly; there was much gaiety, and unbounded hospitality. I have made no disguise of what my opinions upon slavery were, are, and ever must be; but it would be uncandid to deny that the planter in the Southern States has much more in his manner and mode of intercourse that resembles the English country gentleman than any other class of his countrymen; he is more easy, companionable, fond of country life, and out-of-door pursuits. I went with a remarkably agreeable party to spend a day at the rice plantation of one of their chief proprietors; he had the credit of being an excellent manager, and his negroes, young and old, seemed well taken care of and looked after; he repelled the idea—not of educating them—that is highly penal by the law of the State, but of letting them have any religious instruction. I was told by others that there was considerable improvement in this respect. Many whom I met entertained no doubt that slavery would subsist among them for ever; others were inclined to think that it would wear out. While I was willing not to shut my eyes to any of the more favourable external symptoms or mitigations of slavery, other indications could not come across my path without producing deep repugnance. On the very first night of my arrival, I heard the deep sound of a curfew bell: on inquiry I was told, that after it had sounded every night at about nine o'clock, no coloured person, slave or *free* — mark that — might be seen in the streets. One morning, accordingly, I saw a great crowd of coloured persons in the street, and I found they were waiting to see a large number of their colour, who had been taken up the night before on their return from a ball, escorted in their ball dresses from the

Gaol to the Court-house. Indeed, it was almost principally with relation to the free blacks that the anomalous and indefensible working of the system appeared there to develop itself. I was told that the slaves themselves looked down upon the free blacks, and called them rubbish. I must not omit to state that I saw one slave auction in the open street, arising from the insolvency of the previous owner: a crowd stood round the platform, on which sat the auctioneer, and beside him were placed in succession the lots of from one to five negroes. The families seemed to be all put up together, but I imagine they must often be separated; they comprised infants and all ages. As far as I could judge, they exhibited great indifference to their changing destiny. I heard the auctioneer tell one old man, whom I could have hardly distinguished from a white person, that he had been bought by a good master. One could not help shuddering at the future lot of those who were not the subjects of this congratulation.

I went into the Head Court of Justice at Charleston, and found seven persons present; five of them were judges, one was the lawyer addressing them, the other was the opposing counsel, who was walking up and down the room. I attended a meeting of the convention of the Episcopal Church of South Carolina; whether it may be for encouragement or warning to those who wish for the introduction or revival of such synods at home, I mention the point then under discussion; it was how far it was proper to show deference for the opinion of the Bishop.

In point of neatness, cleanliness, and order, the slave-holding States appeared to stand in about the same relation to the free, as Ireland does to England; every thing appears slovenly, ill-arranged, incomplete; windows do not shut, doors do not fasten; there is a superabundance of hands to do every thing, and little is thoroughly done. The country round Charleston for scores, and I believe hundreds of miles, is perfectly flat, and full of swamps, but there I had the first indications of the real genius of the south, in the white houses lined with verandahs, the broad-leaved deep green magnolias and wild orange trees in the gardens, the large yellow jessamine and palmeto in the hedges, and the pendant streamers of grey moss on the under-branches of the rich evergreen live oak, which supplies unrivalled timber for ship-building.

I left Charleston in a small American mail-packet, for the island of Cuba. I must not dwell on the voyage, which, from our being much becalmed, lasted twelve days, double its due; we were long off the low flat coasts of Georgia and Florida, and I felt inclined to say with Goldsmith —

"And wild Altama echoed to our woe."

On the 14th of March we passed under the impregnable rock of the Castle, called the Moro, and, answering the challenge from its terraced battlements, we found ourselves in the unrivalled harbour of the Havana. How enchanting, to the senses at least, were the three weeks I spent in Cuba! How my memory turns to its picturesque forms and balmy skies. During my whole stay, the thermometer scarcely varied from 76° to 78° in the shade. I am disposed to wonder that these regions are not more resorted to by our countrymen for enjoyment of life, and escape from death. Nothing was ever so unlike either Europe or America as the Havana; at least I had never been in Spain, the mother country, which I suppose it most resembles. The courts of the gleaming white houses have a Moorish look, the interiors are much covered with arabesques, and on the outside towards the street they have immense open spaces for windows, in which they generally find it superfluous to put any glass; the carriages are called Volantès, and look as if they had been intended to carry Don Quixote. Then how delicious it used to be, late in the evening, under a moonlight we can scarcely imagine, to sit in the square called the Place of Arms, where in a space flanked by some gleaming palm trees, and four small fountains, a gay crowd listened to excellent music from a Spanish military band. It is certainly the handsomest town I saw in the New World, and gives a great idea of the luxury and splendour of Spain in her palmy days. The billiard rooms and ice-saloons streamed with light; the great theatre is as large and brilliant as almost any in Europe. Again, how full of interest were some visits I paid in the interior, both to Spanish and American households. I cannot condense my impressions of the scenery better than by repeating some short stanzas which with such influences around me I could not help perpetrating. I hope that while they bear witness to the intoxicating effects of the landscape and the climate, they do not wholly leave out of view the attendant moral.

  Ye tropic forests of unfading green,
   Where the palm tapers, and the orange glows,
  Where the light bamboo weaves her feathery screen,
   And her tall shade the matchless seyba throws:

Ye cloudless ethers of unchanging blue,
  Save as its rich varieties give way,
To the clear sapphire of your midnight hue,
  The burnished azure of your perfect day.

Yet tell me not my native skies are bleak,
  That, flushed with liquid wealth, no cane-fields wave;
For Virtue pines, and Manhood dares not speak,
  And Nature's glories brighten round the Slave.

Among the country houses I visited was the sugar estate of one of the chief Creole nobles of the island—(I do not know whether my hearers will be aware that the proper meaning of a Creole is a person of European descent born in America)—I was treated there with the most refined and courteous hospitality; and what a view it was from the terrace of golden cane-fields, and fringing woods, and azure sea! The treatment of the domestic slaves appeared kind and affectionate, and all the negro children on the estate repeated their catechism to the Priest, and were then brought in to dance and romp in the drawing-room. Generally there does not appear to be the same amount of repulsion between the white and coloured races as in the United States, and there is the pleasant spectacle of their being mixed together in the churches. Still the crying, conclusive fact remains, that the average negro population died off in ten years, and had to be recruited by continuous importations, which are so many breaches of the solemn treaties between Spain and us. On one coffee estate which I visited—(and generally the coffee cultivation is far lighter than that of the sugar cane)—a still darker shade was thrown upon the system, as I was told from a most authentic source that there was great difficulty in preventing mothers from killing their offspring. General Valdez, who was Captain-general of the island during my visit, is thought to have exerted himself honestly in putting down the slave trade. I believe it has been as much encouraged as ever under some of his successors. The politics of Cuba are rather delicate ground to tread upon just now, and are likely to be continually shifting; it appeared to me that all the component parties held each other in check, like the people who are all prevented from killing each other in the farce of the Critic. The despotism and exclusiveness of the Mother country were complete; every one gave the same picture of the corruption and demoralization which pervaded every department of administration and justice. The Creoles are prevented from rising against this system, from dread of the negroes rising against them, over and above the large Spanish force always kept on foot there; the Americans, who have got possession of a large proportion of the estates, do not like to hazard any attempt at annexation, without at least adequate aid from other quarters, as they would have to deal with the Spanish army, some of the Creoles, and all the Negroes : and the Negroes, the most deeply wronged party of any, would bring down on themselves in case of any general rising amongst them, the Spaniards, Creoles, Americans within, and Americans without. May the providence of God reserve for these enchanting shores more worthy destinies then they have ever yet enjoyed!

I availed myself of the magnificent accommodation of one of our West India line-of-packet steamers, which deposited us at the mouth of the Mississippi. I repined at the course of the vessel, receding from the sun, and at first I thought everything looked dingy, after the skies and vegetation of the tropics. I missed especially the palm, the cocoa, and the seyba, but there was still the orange tree, and, what they have not in Cuba, the magnolia, a forest tree in full blossom : the sugar plantations of Louisiana seemed kept in very trim order: we passed the ground made memorable by the victory of General Jackson over the English, and soon drew up among the numerous tiers of masts and steam-boats that line the crescent outline of New Orleans.

The good I have to say of New Orleans must be chiefly confined to the St. Charles Hotel, which is the most splendid of its kind that I saw even in the United States. When it is at its full complement 560 dine there every day — 350 of whom sleep in the house; there are 160 servants, 7 French cooks; all the waiters, whites — Irish, English, French, German, and American : the very intelligent proprietor of the hotel told me he thought the Irish made the best; he has them altogether every day at noon, when they go through a regular drill, and rehearse the service of a dinner. Nothing can be more distinct than the appearance of the American and French portions of the town; the American is laid out in broad streets, high houses, and large stores; the French in narrow streets, which suits a warm climate better perhaps, and a great proportion of one-storied houses, which they thought a better security against hurricanes. I spent my time not unpleasantly, particularly two days at the plantation of an opulent proprietor, where the slaves seemed the subject of much thoughtful attention as far as their physical condition is concerned: the weather at this season,—the middle of April, — was delicious, but it is the last place in the world I should choose for a residence. For long periods the climate is most noxious to human life; it is the occasional haunt of the yellow fever, the river runs at a higher level than the town, and the putrid swamp is ever ready to ooze through the thin layer of rank soil above it; and, worse than any merely natural malaria, the dregs of the worst type of the French and American character, notwithstanding the more wholesome elements by which their influence is undoubtedly tempered, impart a moral taint to the social atmosphere.

Though in my journey henceforward I passed over immense spaces, and saw great varieties of scenes and men, yet as it became now more of a matter of real travelling, and did not show me so much of the inner social life, it will be a relief to you to hear, especially after the lengthened trespass I have already made on your attention, that I shall get over the remaining ground far more rapidly. I went from New Orleans to Louisville, on board the *Henry Clay* steamer, 1500 miles, which lasted six days; the first 1100 miles were on the Mississippi. It is impossible to be on the "Father of Waters," as I believe the name denotes, without some emotion; its breadth hardly appears so imposing as that of many far inferior streams; at New Orleans it must be under three-quarters of a mile, but its width rather paradoxically increases as you recede from its mouth; its colour is that of a murky, pulpy, yellowish mud, but still its full, deep, brimming volume pleases, chiefly, I suppose, from the knowledge that thus it rolls on for 5000 miles, and waters a valley capable of feeding the world; there is little break of outline, but the continuous parallel lines of forest are partially dotted, first by the sugar fields of Louisiana, then by the cotton enclosures of the states of Mississippi and Tennessee, then by the rich meadows of Kentucky. For the last 400 miles we left the sovereign river, and struck up the Ohio, christened by the French the "Beautiful River," and deserving the name, from the swelling wooded slopes which fringe its current; its soft native name of Ohio means "the gently flowing." Louisville is a flourishing town. Thence I dived into the interior of Kentucky, and paid a visit of two or three days to Mr. Clay, at his country residence of Ashland. The qualities which rivet the Senate and captivate his adherents, seemed to me both heightened and softened by his frank, courteous, simple intercourse. He lives with his family in a modest house, among fields of deep red soil and the most luxuriant grass, growing under very thriving and varied timber, the oak, sycamore, locust tree, cedar, and that beautiful ornament of American woods, the sugar maple. He likes showing some English cattle. His countrymen seem to be in the habit of calling upon him without any kind of previous introduction. Slavery, generally mild in the pastoral state of Kentucky, was certainly seen here in its least repulsive guise; Mr. Clay's own negro servant, Charles, was much devoted to him; he took him with him on a tour into Canada, and when some abolitionists there wanted him to leave his master, "Not if you were to give me both your Provinces," was the reply.

My next halt was at the White Sulphur Springs in the western portion of Virginia. The season had not yet commenced, early in May, so I was in sole possession of the place. One of my southern friends had kindly placed a delightful little cottage at my disposal, and I enjoyed in the highest degree the unwonted repose in the solitude of virgin forests, and the recesses of the green Alleghanies. Here were my brief Farewell lines to the small temple-like cupola over the bright sulphur well from which I used to drink many times in the day:—

> Hail dome! whose unpresuming circle guards
> Virginia's flowing fountain: still may health
> Hover above thy crystal urn, and bring
> To cheeks unus'd their bloom! may Beauty still
> Sit on thy billowy swell of wooded hills,
> And deep ravines of verdure; may the axe,
> Improvement's necessary pioneer,
> Mid forest solitudes, still gently pierce,
> Not bare their leafy bowers! This votive lay,
> Like wreath of old on thy white columns hung,
> Albeit of scentless flowers from foreign soil,
> Scorn not, and bid the Pilgrim pass in peace.

I had, at this time, much travelling in the stage coaches, and I found it amusing to sit by the different coachmen, who were generally youths from the Eastern States, pushing their way in life, and full of fresh and racy talk. One said to me, lamenting the amount of debt which the State through which we were travelling had incurred, "I suppose your State has no debt," — a compliment I could not quite appropriate. Another, who probably came from New York, where they do not like to use the word Master in speaking of their employers, but prefer an old Dutch name, Boss, said to me, "I suppose the Queen is your Boss now."

I again turned my face to the West, and passed Cincinnati, which, together with all that I saw of the State of Ohio, seemed to me the part of the Union where, if obliged to make the choice, I should like best to fix my abode. It has a great share of all the civilization and appliances of the old settled States of the East, with the richer soil, the softer climate, the fresher spring of life, which distinguish the West. It had besides to me the great attraction of being the first Free State which I reached on my return from the region of slavery; and the contrast in the appearance of prosperity and progress is just what a friend of freedom would always wish it to be. One of my visitors at Cincinnati told me he remembered when the town only contained a few log cabins; when I was there it had 50,000 inhabitants. I shall not easily forget an evening view from a neighbouring hill, over loamy corn-fields, wooded knolls, and even some vineyards, just where the Miami River discharges its gentle stream into the ample Ohio. I crossed the States of Indiana and Illinois, — looked for the first time on the wide level and waving grass of a prairie — stopped a short time at St. Louis, once a French station, now the flourishing capital of the State of Missouri. I passed the greatest confluence of rivers on the face of our globe, where the Mississippi and Missouri blend their giant currents: the whole river ought properly to have gone by the name of the Missouri, as it is by far the most considerable stream, its previous course before the junction exceeding the entire course of the Mississippi, both before and after it; it is the Missouri, too, which imparts its colour to the united stream, and for two or three miles you distinguish its ochre-coloured waters as they line the hitherto clear current of the Upper Mississippi. At Jacksonville, in Illinois, I was told a large colony of Yorkshiremen were settled; and I was the more easily induced to believe it, as it seemed to me about the most thriving and best cultivated neighbourhood I had seen. I embarked at Chicago, on the great lakes: but here I must desist from pursuing my devious wanderings on those large inland seas, and on the opposite shore of Canada. Many thousands of miles have I steamed away over Lakes Michigan, Huron, Erie, Ontario, the Rideau Canal, the St. Lawrence and Ottawa rivers; some of these I traversed twice, and they supplied some of the most interesting and picturesque features of my long journeyings. I should have scrupled in any case to touch upon the politics of Canada, and, indeed, my pauses at any fixed spot were too short to qualify me for the attempt, even if it had been desirable. It is a magnificent region, especially its western portion,—happy in climate, soil, and scenery. I will, however, only attempt to dash off two slight sketches from my Canadian recollections.

Here is the first. I stood in a terraced garden on the summit of a high promontory, running with a steep angle into the basin made by the river St. Lawrence, of which it is no exaggeration to say that the water is as clear, bright, and, above all, green as any emerald; here, upon I believe the most imperial site in the world, stand the citadel and city of Quebec. The shipping was lying in great quantity close under the rocky steep, and was dotted for a considerable way along the shining river. In front was the island of Orleans, well-shaped and full-peopled; ridge upon ridge beyond, ending with Cape Tourment, descended on the river; the shore on either side gleamed with white villages, and the town below seemed to climb, or almost leap, up the straight precipice, broken with high convent-roofs and glittering tinned spires. The flag of England waved upon the highest bastion that crowned the rock; the band of the Queen's Guards was playing in the garden; the clearest blue of western skies was above my head; and, rising above the whole glowing scene, was the commemorative pillar to that General Wolfe, who on this spot transferred to us Englishmen, by his own victory and death, and with the loss of forty-five men, the mastery of a Continent.

The only other scene I will attempt to sketch shall be in the centre of Lake Huron, on one of its countless islands. I am justified in using that epithet, since, not long ago, our Government ordered a survey to be made of the islands; they counted 40,000, and then gave it up, and some of these were of no contemptible size, one of them being ninety miles long. I was one of a party which, at that time, went annually up the lake to attend an encampment of many thousand Indians, and make a distribution of presents among them. About sunset, our flotilla of seven canoes, manned well by Indian and French Canadian crews, drew up, some of the rowers cheering the end of the day's work with snatches of a Canadian boat-song. We disembarked on some rocky islet which, as probably as not, had never felt the feet of man before. In a few moments the utter solitude had become a scene of bustle and business, carried on by the sudden population of some sixty souls; tents had been pitched in which we were to sleep; small trees had been cut for fuel; fires had been lighted, round which the motley crews were preparing the evening meal; some were bathing in the transparent little bays, some standing on a jutting piece of cliff, fishing; and here and there an Indian in the water, motionless, watching with an intent gaze, a spear in his hand ready to dart on his prey beneath. A large oil-cloth had been spread for our party on a convenient ledge of rock; hot peasoup, hot fish, the chase of the day, and large cold rounds of beef, showed that, though we were in the desert, we did not fare like anchorites; and the summer moon rose on the scattered fires, and the gay bivouac, and the snatches of song and chorus that from time to time woke the unaccustomed echoes of Lake Huron.

Entering the United States again, I made a rapid journey by Lakes Champlain and George, by Ticonderoga and Saratoga,—historic names; spent four very delightful days in most attractive society in a New England village, revived the beauteous impressions of the Hudson, and, taking leave of friends not soon to be forgotten, on the quay of New York, left the hospitable shore.

You will have perceived that in these desultory notes I have not attempted to pronounce any formal judgment upon the American people, or the great experiment they are conducting in the face of the world. The extreme diversity of habits, manners, opinions, feelings, race, and origin, in the several parts of the wide extent of country I traversed, would render the difficulty, great in any case, of such an undertaking, still more subtle and complicated. The striking contrasts in such a shifting and variegated aspect of society, make me feel that any such general and dashing summary could only be attempted after the fashion of a passage which I have always much admired in Gibbon, where, wishing to give a fair view of the poetical character of Claudian, he sums up separately his merits and defects, and leaves his reader to strike the just balance. In some such mode it might be stated, that

North America, viewed at first with respect to her natural surface, exhibits a series of scenery, various, rich, and, in some of its features, unparalleled; though she cannot, on the whole, equal Europe in her mountain elevations, how infinitely does she surpass her in rivers, estuaries, and lakes! This variegated surface of earth and water is seen under a sky warm, soft, and balmy in some — clear, blue, and brilliant in all its latitudes, with a transparency of atmosphere which Italy does not reach, with varieties of forest-growth and foliage unknown to Europe, and with a splendour of views in autumn before which painting must despair. With respect to the moral aspect, I naturally feel the difficulty of any succinct or comprehensive summary infinitely heightened. The feature which is the most obvious, and probably the most enviable, is the nearly entire absence, certainly of the appearance, and, in a great degree, of the reality of poverty; in no part of the world, I imagine, is there so much general ease and comfort among the great bulk of the people, and a gushing abundance struck me as the prominent characteristic of the land. It is not easy to describe how far this consideration goes to brighten the face of nature, and give room for its undisturbed enjoyment. Within a mere span of time, as compared with the general growth and progress of nations, the industry, at once steady and persevering, of the inhabitants, has cleared enormous tracts of forest, reared among their untrodden glades spacious and stately cities, opened new highways through the swamp and the desert, covered their unequalled rivers with fleets of steam-boats and craft of every form, given an extension to canals beyond all previous experience, and filled land and water with hardy miracles of successful enterprise. The traveller, wafted with marvellous ease by steam-boats and railways over prodigious spaces, cannot but indulge in what may appear a more superficial satisfaction at the accommodation he meets with in the hotels of the principal cities, which are regulated on a scale, and with a splendour and even cleanliness which he will find scarcely rivalled in the capitals of Europe. However absorbed in the pursuits of business, agriculture and trade, the citizens of these young republics may be, and though it would seem to be their obvious vocation in life to cultivate almost boundless wastes, and connect almost interminable distances, circles are nevertheless to be found among them which, in point of refined and agreeable intercourse, of literary taste, and general accomplishment, it would be difficult for the same capitals of the elder world to surpass; the Bench and Bar, as well as other professions, can boast both of the solid and brilliant qualities by which they are adorned; and while much occurs in Congress, that must be deemed rough and unseemly, the chords of high and generous feeling are frequently struck within its walls to accents of noble eloquence; in the universal fluency of their public speaking, they undoubtedly surpass ourselves. In rural life, I doubt whether the world can produce more examples of quiet simplicity and prosperous content than would be found, I might say most prominently, in the embowered villages of New England, or the sunny valleys of Pennsylvania. I am sure that I am not wanting in respect for our own operative classes; but neither can I conceal from myself that the appearance of the female factory population of Lowell presents some points of favourable contrast. Among the more opulent portion of society, an idle man without regular profession or fixed pursuit is the exception which excites observation and surprise. The purity of the female character stands deservedly high, and society has been deemed by some to be rendered less agreeable by the rigid devotion of the young married women to their households and nurseries. It is something to have travelled nearly over the whole extent of the Union without having encountered a single specimen either of servility or incivility of manner; by the last I intend to denote intentional rudeness. Elections may seem the universal business, topic, and passion of life, but they are, at least with but few exceptions, carried on without any approach to tumult, rudeness, or disorder; those which I happened to see were the most sedate, unimpassioned processes I can imagine. In the Free States, at least, the people at large bear an active, and, I believe, on the whole, a useful part in all the concerns of internal government and practical daily life; men of all classes, and especially of the more wealthy and instructed, take a zealous share in almost every pursuit of usefulness and philanthropy; they visit the hospitals and asylums; they attend the daily instructions of the schools; they give lectures at Lyceums and Institutes. I am glad to think that I may be treading in their foot-steps on this occasion. I have already mentioned with just praise, the universal diffusion and excellent quality of popular education, as established especially in the States of New England, the powerful Empire State of New York, and, I may add, the prosperous and aspiring State of Ohio. Without venturing to weigh the preponderating recommendations or deficiencies of the Voluntary System, I may fairly ask, what other communities are so amply supplied with the facilities of public worship for all their members? The towns, old and young, bristle with churches; they are almost always well filled; the Sabbath, in the Eastern and Northern States at least, is scrupulously observed; and with the most unbounded freedom of conscience, and a nearly complete absence of polemical strife and bitterness, there is apparently a close unity of feeling and practice in rendering homage to God.

Though it would appear difficult, and must certainly be ungracious, to paint the reverse side of such a country and such a people, a severe observer would not be long at fault. With respect to their scenery itself, while he could not deny that within its vast expanse it contained at times both sublimity and beauty, he might establish against it a charge of monotony, to which the immense continuities of the same surfaces, whether of hill, valley, wood, lake, or river — the straight unbroken skirt of forest, the entire absence of single trees, the square parellelograms of the cleared spaces, the uniform line of zig-zag fences, the staring squareness of the new wooden houses, all powerfully contribute. In regard to climate, without dwelling on such partial influences as the malària which desolates the stunted pine-barrens of North Carolina, and banishes every white native of South Carolina from their rice-plains during the entire summer, the hot damps which festoon the trees on the southern coast with a funereal drapery of grey moss, the yellow fever which decimates the Quays of New Orleans, and the feverish agues which line the banks of the Mississippi, it would be impossible to deny the violent alternations of temperature which have a more general prevalence; and it is certain that much fewer robust forms and ruddy complexions are to be seen than in our own more even latitudes. Passing from the physical to the moral atmosphere, amidst all the vaunted equality of the American freemen, there seemed to be a more implicit deference to custom, a more passive submission to what is assumed to be the public opinion of the day or hour, than would be paralleled in many aristocratic or even despotic communities. This quiet acquiescence in the prevailing tone, this complete abnegation of individual sentiment, is naturally most perceptible in the domain of politics: but

I thought that it also in no inconsiderable degree pervaded the social circle, biassed the decisions of the judicial bench, and even infected the solemn teachings of the pulpit. To this source may probably in some measure be traced the remarkable similarity in the manners, deportment, conversation, and tone of feeling, which has so generally struck travellers from abroad in American society. Who that has seen, can ever forget the slow and melancholy silence of the couples who walk arm-in-arm to the tables of the great hotels, or of the unsocial groups who gather round the greasy meals of the steam-boats, lap up the five minutes' meal, come like shadows, so depart? One of their able public men made an observation to me, which struck me as pungent, and perhaps true, that it was probably the country in which there was less misery and less happiness than in any other of the world. There are other points of manners on which I am not inclined to dilate, but to which it would at least require time to be reconciled: I may just intimate that their native plant of tobacco lies at the root of much that we might think objectionable. However necessary and laudable the general devotion to habits of industry and the practical business of life may be, and though there are families and circles in which no grace, no charm, no accomplishment, are wanting, yet it cannot be denied, that among the nation at large, the empire of dollars, cents, and material interests, holds a very preponderating sway, and that art and all its train of humanities exercise at present but an enfeebled and restricted influence. If we ascend from social to political life, and from manners to institutions, we should find that the endless cycles of electioneering preparations and contests, although they may be carried on for the most part without the riotous turbulence, or overt bribery, by which they are sometimes but too notoriously disgraced among ourselves, still leave no intermission for repose in the public mind; enter into all the relations of existence; subordinate to themselves every other question of internal and foreign policy; lead their public men—I will not say their best, but the average of them—to pander to the worst prejudices, the meanest tastes, the most malignant resentments of the people; at each change of administration incite the new rulers to carry the spirit of proscription into every department of the public service, from the Minister at a great foreign court, to the post-master of some half-barbarous out-post, — thus tending to render those whose functions ought to withdraw them the most completely from party influences the most unscrupulous partisans; and would make large masses welcome war and even acquiesce in ruin, if it appeared that they could thus counteract the antagonist tactics, humiliate the rival leader, or remotely influence the election of the next President. It is already painfully felt that as far as the universal choice of the people was relied on to secure for the highest office of the state the most commanding ability or the most signal merit, it may be pronounced to have failed. There may be less habitual and actual noise in Congress than in our own Parliament, but the time of the House of Representatives, not without cost to the constituent body which pays for their services, is continuously taken up, when not engrossed by a speech of some days' duration, with wrangles upon points of order and angry recriminations; the language used in debate has occasionally sounded the lowest depths of coarse and virulent acrimony, and the floor of the Legislative Hall has actually been the scene of violent personal rencounter. The manners of the barely civilized West, where it has been known that counsel challenge judges on the Bench, and Members of the Legislature fire off rifles at the Speaker as he sits in the chair, would appear to be gradually invading the very inner shrine of the Constitution. Having done justice to the strictness and purity of morals which distinguish many of the more settled portions of the continent, it cannot be concealed that the reckless notions an dhabits of the vagrant pioneers of the West, evinced as these are by the practices of gambling, drinking, and licentiousness, by an habitual disregard of the Sabbath, and by more constant swearing than I ever heard any where else, fearfully disfigure that great valley of the Mississippi, destined inevitably, at no distant day, to be the preponderating section of the entire Union. It is at this day impossible to go into any society, especially of the older and more thoughtful men, some of whom may themselves have borne an eminent part in the earlier struggles and service of the commonwealth, without hearing the degeneracy of modern times, and the downward tendency of all things, despondingly insisted upon. At the period of my visit, besides the numerous instances of individual bankruptcy and insolvency, not, alas, peculiar to the New World, the doctrine of repudiation, officially promulgated by sovereign States, had given an unpleasing confirmation to what is perhaps a prevailing tendency among retired politicians. I have reserved for the last topic of animadversion the crowning evil—the capital danger—the mortal plague-spot—Slavery. I have not disclaimed the original responsibility of my own country in introducing and riveting it upon her dependencies ; I do not disguise the portentous difficulties in the way of adequate remedy to the great and growing disease. But what I cannot shut my eyes on is, that while it lasts, it must still continue, in addition to the actual amount of suffering and wrong which it entails on the enslaved, to operate with terrible re-action on the dominant class, to blunt the moral sense, to sap domestic virtue, to degrade independent industry, to check the onward march of enterprise, to sow the seeds of suspicion, alarm, and vengeance in both internal and external intercourse, to distract the national councils, to threaten the permanence of the Union, and to leave a brand, a bye-word, and a jest, upon the name of Freedom.

Having thus endeavoured, without consciousness of any thing mis-stated or exaggerated, though of much that is wanting and incomplete, on either side, to sum up the good and the bad, I leave my hearers to draw their own conclusions from the whole ; there are large materials both for approval and attack, ample grounds both for hope and fear. Causes are occasionally at work which almost appear to portend a disruption of the Federal Union ; at the same time a strong sentiment of pride about it, arising partly from an honest patriotism, partly from a feeling of complacency in its very size and extent, may tend indefinitely to postpone any such pregnant result; but whatever may be the solution of that question, whatever the issue of the future destinies assigned to the great American Republic, it is impossible to have contemplated her extent, her resources, the race that has mainly peopled her, the institutions she has derived or originated, the liberty which has been their life-blood, the industry which has been their offspring, and the free Gospel which has been published on her wide plains and wafted by her thousand streams, without nourishing the belief, and the hope, that it is reserved for her to do much, in the coming generations, for the good of man and the glory of God.

ADDRESSES.

DISTRIBUTION OF PRIZES AT HUDDERSFIELD COLLEGE.

(December, 1843.)

LADIES AND GENTLEMEN,

Though this is the first time that I have had the gratification of attending any meeting in connection with the Huddersfield College, yet you must give me leave to assure you that it has so happened, not from any want of friendly invitation on the part of its friends and supporters, or from the want of any good will or interest on my part. Hitherto, parliamentary and official duties, and such material hindrances as the interposition of seas, whether the Irish Channel, or, more recently, the Atlantic Ocean, have prevented my complying both with their friendly summons and with my own strong inclination; but I have taken advantage of the first opportunity of unengrossed leisure which I have enjoyed in the county of York, to attend the half-yearly examination of the Huddersfield College. There is much in the design and in the constitution of this establishment—there is much in my judgment at least—which entitles it to warm sympathy and active support. My own prepossessions—prejudices, if you like to call them—have been long powerfully associated with the ancient endowed institutions, generally called the great public schools of this country; but I have been long convinced, that in many portions of our land, especially in districts like this, where a long course of successful industry and enterprise has drawn together large masses of people, and has elevated many of them, I do not say to any overweening luxury and opulence, but to honourable and dignified competence, it was most expedient that the means of useful and liberal education should be brought near to their own doors and homes, and that a system should be introduced in which scarcely any of the polite and humanizing branches of study should be omitted, but, in addition to this, more of a practical character, as well as of a comprehensive range, should be given to the customary methods of instruction. I rejoice to perceive in the plan and the very fundamental constitution of this establishment, a full admission of the principle, — of the indispensable principle, in my view, — that all acquirements should be grounded on a religious basis; and I am equally impressed with the urgency, that in any new system aiming at general utility, placed not merely in such districts as that to which I have adverted, but subsisting in such times as those we live in, its benefits should not be fenced in by any exclusive barriers, or founded upon any denominational tests. I do not mean to depreciate the immense importance of our own conscientious convictions; but while I would never discountenance adherence to our own sense of right and duty, I would most strongly recommend the establishment of such institutions, as, without wounding the susceptibilities of the individual conscience, will give the fullest participation of their common benefits to all who may be disposed to enjoy them; and, indeed, I feel no surprise, from knowing those by whom this Institution was mainly founded, and upon looking round me, as at this day, upon many by whom it is still upheld and fostered, that I can trace in the constitution and character of this establishment no deviation from the great principles of religious freedom. Depend upon it, there is no more fitting and genial shelter under which all sound and useful studies, and ornamental accomplishments, can thrive and spread, protecting them alike from the chilling and nipping blight of indifference, and from the blasting breath of bigotry; and tempering habits of independence and self-relying thought with profound humility for that which is supreme, and with tenderness and reverence for the conscientious convictions of others.

I should now just wish, with your kind allowance, to address one or two words of sympathy and counsel to the younger portion of the audience, to those who are the peculiar subjects of the exhibition of this morning. I feel that I may spare all congratulation to the actual receivers of the prizes — to the victors in the lettered ring. The palm that has been assigned to them in the face of an interested and applauding auditory, must be quite sufficient reward in itself, and they will not want any words of mine to enhance it. What I want all, whether successful or unsuccessful competitors, to remember, is, that the acquisition of knowledge is its own chief reward. It is to be valued mainly not for the light in which it exhibits us before others, or the position in which it places us in society, but for what it makes us in ourselves—susceptible of what is beautiful, pursuers of what is useful, practisers of what is right, masters of ourselves, and beyond and above the reach of circumstances. In this attempt to enumerate the proper and best results which can be derived from the acquisition of knowledge, I intend to include all its branches—from the highest and most indispensable, to what are considered the more practical and common-place, or the mere subsidiary and ornamental. None of them, in their several spheres and degrees, ought to be overlooked or slighted. When I allude to high and spiritual matters as the most indispensable, I hope I sufficiently indicate my own meaning. Take away the higher truths, and the most practical pursuits are but labour in vain, and the most graceful acquirements are but fading wreaths hung round empty bowers. But in just subordination to these, I am very glad to observe that considerable attention is bestowed upon what are called classical studies, the knowledge of the Greek and Latin languages, and others. Perhaps you will think that in this observation I am betraying some of the prepossessions or prejudices connected with my own early education, to which I before adverted; but I am most deeply persuaded, that a knowledge and acquaintance with the immortal works contained in those languages,—not, however, I admit, to be too exclusively, or encroachingly, or universally insisted upon,—tend more, perhaps, than any thing else, to train the judgment in composition and criticism, to refine and educate the general taste, and to give at once vigour and grace to literature and to thought; not to mention the never failing sources of refreshment and delight which they secure to their individual votaries. If I do not refer so pointedly to what may be considered the more useful and practical branches of study, whether you include the knowledge of modern languages, the mastery of all resources of arithmetic, and the rudiments of the leading sciences, it is not from underrating their great and prominent importance, but because their advantages, though immense, are of a more obvious character. They come home almost to all our pursuits and occupations, and cross us in almost every path of life. Well, then, my young friends, if you will allow me to turn myself to you,—when the motives for diligent application are so varied and important, when the returns to it are so sure and so promising,—for though we hear very often of bad bargains and ruinous speculations, yet I feel sure, however long your life may be, you will hardly, in the course of it, ever meet with a man who will tell you that he regrets the time which he has spent in the acquisition of knowledge, or repents of having become a scholar,—resolve now, if you never did so before, not to lose those precious hours, the weight of which may be prized in gold, while they have the speed and lightness of feathers ; and most of all, I wish you to prize beyond all other acquisitions — beyond the acquisition of learning, however solid, or the mastery of accomplishments, however brilliant ; prize before them all, the formation of individual character, the building up of moral habits, the whole pervading discipline of duty. Join docility and teachableness in your studies to that independence and resolution of will, which will enable you to apply and to appropriate to yourselves the teachings of others' wisdom, and the lessons of your own experience; so that when the time shall come for your leaving the friendly shelter of this institution, and for launching out your small barks into the wide and stormy sea of life, you may not only carry with you those honourable certificates of approval of your past exertions and conduct, which I have had the satisfaction of delivering to two of your number this day, but you may go forth into the busy arena of the world, and there, whatever may be your special calling,—in literature and art, in science or in business, amidst public avocations or among family connections,—you may at last, one and all of you, be fitted and prepared to play the part of useful Christian citizens.

I would now only gently remind even those who have so honourably come forward in support of this institution, that while they desire to promote the cause of a creditable and liberal education amongst those members of society for whom it is calculated, they must not forget, that in these times it is most indispensable to the welfare and even to the salvation of the country at large, that the benefits of education should not be confined to any particular class of persons ; but that they should be extended to every species of occupation, and to every department of society. Given already to the nobles, to the merchants, to the master manufacturers, they ought not to be withheld from the mechanic, the labourer, and the cottager. You have made ample and splendid provision in order to meet the exigencies of those that are, comparatively speaking, in easier circumstances, and in so doing you have done most wisely, and most well. May those classes enjoy and appropriate the advantages thus held out to them; may we hear of your sons giving themselves up with ardour to all the studies of this place; may they delight in the sublime lay of Homer, and the faultless line of Virgil; may they obtain a proficiency in every polite and graceful accomplishment, or wing their adventurous flight through the highest realms of science! But while they do all this, be it our care also to provide that, if you will, a plainer, but still a sound and substantial, nourishment shall be afforded to the bulk of the nation, to those who make the pith and marrow of our people. See that it is put within their reach; see that it offers itself to their notice; see that it wooes their acceptance; even let it be pressed upon them, though they should at first sight seem unwilling to take advantage of it. While you support Academies and Colleges, give your assistance and your countenance also to working mens' classes, and to Mechanics' Institutes. While you amply uphold the credit of Huddersfield College, promote also the prosperity of the day-school, and the Sunday-school. Let education be provided for the heirs of poverty and the children of toil, as a genial relaxation from the weary hours of labour; let it be provided for them as a solid and sustaining nurture for the intellectual, the moral, and the spiritual cravings of their nature. And let me give this parting exhortation to you,—that within the whole range of your several spheres, according to the best of your abilities, you should promote the united cause of a free conscience and an universal education.

YORKSHIRE UNION OF MECHANICS' INSTITUTES.

(*Wakefield, May,* 1844.)

IT has so happened, that although I have long been most fully alive to the great utility and advantage of the institutions which generally go by the name of Mechanics' Institutes, this is the very first time at which I have been able to attend the regular proceedings of a Mechanics' Institution within the county of York. To the members, indeed, of these Institutes, to the great body of the mechanics of the West Riding of Yorkshire, I may flatter myself that I am not wholly a stranger; many of us have met upon other occasions, and upon a different stage; but however important such occasions may have been, and however interesting or lofty the themes which belonged to those other theatres of action, a gathering like that of this evening has one evident superiority; it embraces no topics of difference, it marshals us into no opposite ranks of party or denomination, it has nothing to do with conflict; all it has to do with is co-operation. I look upon Mechanics' Institutes as both a creation and a type of the days in which we live; the influences of which they were born, and of which they breathe, are wholly of modern growth. The time was when, in the immediate neighbourhood of the place where we are now met, the opposing armies of the rival Roses were drawn up in menacing array, and soon mixed in murderous conflict; but now, gentlemen, instead of such a competition between us and our good brethren of Lancaster, the objects of our rivalry are, the number and excellence of our respective Mechanics' Institutes; this is, you will agree with me, a far better sight to exhibit in the eyes of heaven and the world than the brawls between the troopers of Warwick and the retainers of Clifford, when Baron was hewing at Baron, and Franklin hacking at Franklin. These revolting scenes, however, have left no other memorial than the exquisite little chapel on the bridge which spans your now peaceful Calder, raised to make propitiation for the souls of the slaughtered; and the days of the Barons have become the days of Mechanics' Institutes. Not that the one came in immediate succession to the other. After what may be especially called the feudal era, there came gradually the days of industry and enterprise, of the stout labourer, and ingenious artificer, and busy trader, and active merchant; nor can we say that their day is yet over, nor must we wish it to be over. No; by the activity of our enterprise and the energy of our industry we have raised a population so vast, and reared a dominion so mighty, that we cannot stop, even if we would; and the wealth which may have once been only considered as the glittering prize of ambition, has become a condition and a necessity even of our national existence. But within a period of almost the youngest life amongst us, new influences have been brought to bear, especially, on the working and industrious classes of the community; a new spirit has been breathed into the dry frame of trade and enterprise; and the education, and the accompanying knowledge, which formerly only graced, and that sometimes very superficially, the more privileged and opulent members of the community in the warehouse and counting-house, have now struck their kindly roots deeper down, and visited the mechanic at his workshop, and the weaver at his loom. Instead of merely impregnating the upper layers of the mass, they have penetrated, and warmed, and vivified the whole body beneath. In the process of this, I will not say, revolution, because the word sometimes conveys the idea of something violent, formidable, and convulsive; but of this great social recovery, this gradual and genial progress, Mechanics' Institutes and similar institutions have borne a conspicuous and most creditable part, and in the furtherance of Mechanics' Institutes, as in other good things, the men of Yorkshire may claim a very honourable share. Why, they produced from among them Dr. Birkbeck, who I believe may be justly considered their original founder; and they honoured, in the election of Lord Brougham, one of their most efficient patrons and supporters. I say nothing of those who are now prominently engaged in this good field of action. It is, therefore, with much pleasure that I witness such a meeting as this, which, to say nothing of its more ornamental portion, comprises not only so goodly an assembly of the members and mechanics of this fair city of Wakefield, but shows, by the number of representatives and delegates which it has brought together from other similar bodies within the Riding, that there is a sort of corporate life among you, not perhaps equally vivacious and mettlesome in all the limbs, but still ready to feel sympathy, and to communicate energy; to assist the struggles of the weak, and to applaud the success of the strong. May this wholesome and precious rivalry long continue, in which, while it will be an honour to be first, it will yet be a pleasure to be outstripped! In truth, the circumstances of this great district ought to command the general prevalence and hearty support of institutions of this character; you have here the large accumulation of great masses of people; you have a great diversity and keen competition of employments, exciting ingenuity, and stimulating discovery; the nature of your occupations is such as to call for all that can be procured in the way of refreshment and relaxation. In your busy and engrossing occupations, toiling at your daily task, and for your daily bread, you may certainly be without those opportunities and aids to advancement in study or in discovery which belong to studious ease, or to learned leisure; but it is not from these quarters that the most brilliant contributions to human advancement have been always made ; it was not from these classes that Watt, or Brindley, or Fulton, or Burns, or Chantrey, came. In my travels on the great continent of North America, I chanced to fall in with a blacksmith in one of the interior States, who, while he most assiduously performed all the requirements of his calling, accomplished the mastery of, so as to be perfectly able to read, about fifty languages. I have just put down an extract which was made from the journal of this blacksmith linguist ; it is a diary of his daily business for five days taken by chance in the course of the year. The extract is from the commonplace book of Elihu Burritt, in 1838. " June 5th. Read fifty lines of Hebrew, thirty-seven of Celtic; six hours of forging. June 6th. Read thirty-seven lines of Hebrew, forty of Celtic ; six hours of forging. June 7th. Read sixty lines of Hebrew, sixty lines of Celtic, fifty-four pages of French, twenty names of stars; five hours of forging. June 8th. Read fifty-one lines of Hebrew, fifty lines of Celtic, forty pages of French, fifteen names of stars ; eight hours of forging. June 10th (Sunday). 100 lines of Hebrew, eighty-five pages of French, four services at church, Bible-class at noon." For many days he was unwell, and sometimes worked twelve hours at the forge; so that it seems that he did not come within the Ten-hours bill. Now, lest you should be tempted to think that the concerns of his handicraft interfered with or were prejudicial to his course of study, I shall subjoin a remark which was made with respect to him by Mr. Combe, the eminent phrenologist, who travelled in America, and who gave the greatest attention to the developments of the human head, and to the conditions of human health. Mr. Combe says : " One thing is obvious, that the necessity for forging saved this student's life ; if he had not been forced by necessity to labour, he would in all probability have devoted himself so incessantly to his books, that he would have ruined his health, and been carried to a premature grave." So you perceive that work may not only be no drawback but even an assistance to the most intense literary labour: the patient achievements of well-directed industry, and the heaven-kindled flame of genius, are confined to no order of our fellow-men, and are denied to none. The Mechanics' Institute is quite as likely as the country churchyard to produce,

> " Hands that the rod of empire might have swayed,
> Or waked to ecstacy the living lyre."

But then, if it does produce them, it is much more likely to discover them, develop them, and to give them to mankind ; if we do produce them, we will not keep our Miltons "mute and inglorious," as they were in the churchyard. As for our "village Hampdens," I do not know what we can do with them. I hope I say it without offence to a very excellent and kind-hearted neighbour of yours, I do not know what else we can do with them than send them to protect Heath Common against its threatened inclosure. For these reasons, as well as for many more that have been often better said, I do hope that all whom I now address, and all whom my words may in any way reach, will continue and extend their support of all Mechanics' Institutes within their neighbourhood and influence. They will do well to attend to all suggestions respecting improved methods and enlarged means for instruction and enjoyment which the progress of time and the increased attention given to the whole subject will be continually supplying. I need not caution you not to make your proceedings too frivolous, or occasions either for idle dissipation or boisterous clamour ; but neither would I have you make them too grave and stiff. You may generally mix the acquisition of sound knowledge and rational improvement with social enjoyment, with occasional merry-making, with all that lights a smile on the brow of care, throws a spell over the weariness of labour, or promotes mutual good will and neighbourly heartiness ; nor need I add, that, although in the remarks which I have made I have confined myself to what seemed the direct object of these institutions, that is, the promotion of useful knowledge and the pursuit of rational enjoyment, I might remind you that, while all kinds of knowledge are useful, there is one, and perhaps only one, which is absolutely needful ; and while of all knowledge we are told that it shall vanish away, of Christianity we know that it never faileth.

LEEDS MECHANICS' INSTITUTION.

(*February*, 1845.)

Mr. Chairman, Ladies, and Gentlemen,

Even without the very friendly introduction of your chairman (Mr. E. Baines), I should have felt that I did not present myself before you as an absolute stranger. When I have come before you, it has generally been under the pressure of some exciting topics of the moment, and also at periods when I could not hope to chime in with the unanimous feeling of all who might hear me. On the occasion of our present meeting, though our topics are not deficient in interest or in dignity, yet I am happy to feel that they are calm, conciliating, and combining; and that not one person whom I have the pleasure to address, probably, will find any opinion of his ruffled by any counter-sentiment which I may have to offer. That the constitution and purpose of your society—the object and spirit which has brought together this intelligent and genial assembly—exactly falls in with all my sympathies, and stirs up all my warmest interest, it will be almost superfluous in me to declare. If I wanted testimony to the value of such institutions, I do not think that it could have been borne in a more interesting or striking manner than in the address which you have just heard from your late honorary secretary, Mr. Kitson, who, in addition to the happy and encouraging results which he has observed in others, tells you, with all the force and warmth of his own consciousness and his own gratitude, that if it had not been for the Mechanics' Institution, he probably would not have stood before you in the same honourable position, and in the same creditable sphere of society, which he now fills. I should feel the utility and importance of such an institution in any place whatsoever; but I feel them most abundantly in this busy city, in this populous district, in this stirring hive of industry and enterprise, amid these bristling stacks of chimneys, this roaring clatter of wheels, this ceaseless hum of tongues, this wear and tear of human life. Do not think that in any of the expressions that I have used I mean to depreciate the dignity of labour, or to rob it of any of its well-won honours. On the contrary, when your chairman was talking just now of temples erected by the pagan population of Rome to Virtue and to Honour, I cannot help feeling that if I had lived in the old times of mythology, almost the first power to which I should have been willing to pay divine honours would have been Labour. Indeed, of all the heathen gods and goddesses, by far the most creditable character seems to me to have been Vulcan, who went hammering on in his sooty forge, while the rest of them either indulged themselves in idle dissipation, or were engaged in slaughtering the unhappy mortals supposed to be subject to their caprice. If I wanted to cite a testimony and an evidence of the magic power of labour, and of the mode in which it can alter the whole surface, and transmute the entire substance, of the matter on which it acts, I think I might adduce as my proof the contrast of the times when your forefathers met to transact the business of the year under the old oak of Skyrack, or when the cloth market of Leeds was held upon the bridge, and the clothiers exposed their goods upon its battlements; and of these our own times, when every hill and valley teem with life and occupation; when the moorland is turned into hamlets, and every hamlet has become a town, large and important in itself; and the rustic lanes of olden times are transformed into crowded thoroughfares and busy markets, where the interchanges of a wide-spread commerce are being passed and repassed in their perpetual current; where the fleeces of the Elbe, or the Crimea, or Australia, are mixed up with our home-grown "noils and shorts;" and whence the products of your looms and your workshops are sent forth to clothe the freed inhabitants of the West India Islands, or the countless hordes of the farthest China. I am, indeed, far from belonging to that fond, and, as I think, rather foolish school, which is always looking wistfully back to the past, and thinking that our sires had a better job of it than ourselves. I am, indeed, far from questioning that this school comprises many very able and amiable men. At the same time, I own that "Young England" has rather too much of Old England for me. I cordially believe that, on the whole, this is the time, and this is the country, to live in. When I say this, I am far from meaning that all is just as it should be. I know that there is much which is amiss, and which needs to be set right. There are our dwellings,—sewerage,—the supply of water, of air, of light,—improvement in education, both in quantity and quality. Above all, there is a deep, stagnant mass of poverty, which needs to be moved, and sifted, and uplifted. But still, making all due allowance for these real and unquestionable drawbacks, I believe that there never was a community like that which an eminent and lamented writer, the late Dr. Arnold, termed "this kingly commonwealth of England," —there never was a period like the present, which afforded more food for every appetite of manly intellect, and more scope for every exercise of active virtue. I believe there is scarcely anything which might not be attained, if we could only one and all of us determine to rise up to what we might be; if it could only be felt thoroughly by every one of us, no matter how humble his place, or how contracted his sphere, that each one has his own appointed work and mission,—not, assuredly, by indulging in any puffed-up opinion of his own capacity, and endeavouring to escape from his natural place or his allotted business, but by constant and conscientious perseverance, in which he might do much, very much, to smooth all the troubled elements of the daily life around him, and to aid the general welfare and advancement of his species. I believe that there is nothing at once so ambitious, and yet so humble, as duty; and it is the true, the practical, the Christian philosophy to endeavour rightly to apportion and attemper the ambition and the humility. It is because I believe that labour affords the main occasion and chief exercise-ground of duty, and because I see what labour has already done, and stretch my eyes forward to the yet greater things which it has to do in the world, that I said that if I had lived in the olden times, I should have been ready to build temples and altars in its name. But when I give this merited praise to labour, I believe, at the same time, that, with a view to the interests of labour itself, with a view to its vigorous, and permanent, and cheerful exercise, we ought not to exact too excessive and engrossing a service; but that breaks and relaxations are desirable, and salutary, and even necessary, to its own proper development and support. It is, therefore, that I love to read occasionally of the expeditions made by the Monster trains which convey large numbers far away from the smoke and confinement of their own streets and shops, to see whatever may be worthy of note, upon the many points of that great net-work of railways by which we are in the process of being surrounded,—to the crowded quays of Liverpool or the gothic aisles of York; and I should not repine—let me say it with the peace of Mr. Wordsworth—if a protracted line of railway should, on some sunny afternoon, carry a large bevy of the tradesmen of Leeds to the soft margin of Windermere or Ullswater. It is on the same ground that it has given me peculiar pleasure to have the privilege of witnessing and sharing the celebration of this evening, in the midst of such a community as I have already adverted to, and in the presence of such a company as that which I now see around me. It has, indeed, fallen to my lot often to be present at what are termed fashionable amusements in various quarters of the globe, and I have always found that they are pretty much the same thing wherever in the world it might be—whether amongst the courtier circles of St. Petersburgh, or the republican dandies of New York. I do not mean to assume any very severe or moralizing tone with respect to the attempts of people to amuse or enliven themselves, but I must say that I have generally found these very polished amusements to be rather listless, unmeaning, and unsatisfying things, where people seemed to come because they had nothing better to do, and to find it a great relief when it was time to go away. But an assembly like this, confined to no class or walk in life, comprising very many of what are termed the middle and labouring classes of society, those who keep the business of daily life really going, brought and kept together by no other tie than the love of knowledge, the wish to attain it and to communicate it, to acquire for themselves and to dispense to others the reciprocal benefits of instruction and advancement—this, to say nothing of its being more useful and more ennobling, seems to me a far fresher, livelier, heartier thing, than the high-flying entertainments I have adverted to,—the morning battue or the midnight polka. The constitution of your society seems to me to embrace all the objects which it must have been designed to accomplish. I am glad to hear from the lips of your respected chairman that it has lately been growing by hundreds, and I hope the time is coming when it is to increase by thousands. The purposes which it effects seem to me to supply a suitable and harmless relaxation to the strain of daily toil, and a pleasant variety and stimulus to what is, perhaps, even worse than the strain and severity of toil, the sameness of habitual routine. The mechanic or the operative, shut up during the day within the precincts of the shop, or with his ear dulled with the recurring sound of his shuttle, may here learn something of that Nature from the personal observation of which he is, in a great measure, debarred; and something of the past history of his country, to whose wealth and power his industry and enterprise make no mean contribution; or something of the links which attach him to higher and more enduring destinies. The delivery of oral lectures and the communication of original papers appear to me to be a most valuable supplement to the hoarded treasures of past wisdom and genius which are stored in the volumes of your libraries. On looking over your report, I was greatly struck with the interesting subjects which formed the materials of the lectures and papers which have been read and delivered during the last year; and I now rejoice to find that your chairman himself shortly meditates to give you a history of the invention of that art of printing, which, in its maturity, has been so honourably illustrated by the name he bears. If I had to choose one of the most encouraging and gratifying circumstances of the times in which we live,—if I were asked the feature in them upon which I should be inclined to dwell with most of complacency and hope, I should not select even the expansion of commerce, or the revival of trade, little as I should be disposed, anywhere, and least of all in this neighbourhood, or this society, to undervalue the numberless direct or indirect advantages connected with these considerations; nor yet the increase of our naval force, though I concur in the probable expediency of such a step; nor still the wisdom of any of the provisions of the recent budget, for which I trust I may be allowed to do justice even to a political opponent: but it would be the manifest increase and development of that kindly and considerate spirit, which in so many quarters and in so many directions seems to be guiding many of the wealthier and more educated classes to improve, cheer, and elevate the condition, to consult the present comfort—and the abiding welfare of their worse-provided and destitute brethren. I do not seek to attach an exaggerated or undue importance to any single measure or undertaking of the sort—public libraries in one place, public laundries in another, public walks and parks in a third. I know that wisdom is not always inseparably to be found even in a library, and that health cannot be commanded in every case, even by the Hydropathic establishment of Ben Rhydding. But I believe all these measures to be useful as auxiliaries; I believe them to be conceived in a right spirit, and to be directed with a proper aim. I know that the mass of penury and wretchedness which occasionally may fester in your streets and wound the eye of day, or else shrink to pine and perish in the shade—and I am sorry to observe that the recent experience of some of you bears witness to these dark truths—I know that this unsightly and gloomy mass cannot be raised by any single wrench of the lever, or be moved by the prowess of a single arm; but if a persevering, and discerning, and conscientious benevolence will keep itself fixed to the work,—if it will stretch out its many and far-reaching hands, loaded with the supplies for all the necessities of mankind—food for their hunger, medicine for their sickness, air and light for their dwellings, culture and instruction for their ignorance, relaxation for their long weary spells of toil, the vigour and buoyancy that wait upon that blessed thing called progress, there is nothing that I would despair of, from the efforts of the enlightened sagacity of our day, ministering the charity of the Gospel. I do not wish to arrogate too high or solemn a character for our present proceedings, or for the gathering of to-night, but I believe them to be subsidiary to the graver duties and sterner business of life. Looked upon in that light, I believe such meetings and such institutions to be conducive to sound information, to refined accomplishment, to social enjoyment, to mental and to moral progress; and thus esteeming them, I have no hesitation in giving, and in commending to your favourable acceptance, "Prosperity to the Leeds Mechanics' Institution and Literary Society."

SUNDAY SCHOOL JUBILEE.
Halifax, June, 1846.

LADIES AND GENTLEMEN,

I am extremely obliged to you for the great kindness and warmth of your welcome to me. I must state to you, that I come before you, at present, in rather a chance or haphazard manner, and it was a very sudden thought my finding myself able to be here at all; so that I am by no means able to address you in anything like a prepared or premeditated harangue. But knowing that you were to meet this evening, and having been favoured with an invitation to be present on the occasion, I could not forego the sincere gratification which it gives me to find myself among such an assembly, upon such an occasion, and at the close of such an exhibition as we have beheld this morning. I was very sorry indeed to be prevented by an inevitable engagement from witnessing more of that interesting and elevating spectacle than I did, as I only came in at what may be called the tail of it; but I did see enough, and I did hear enough, to convey impressions which I feel assured will remain to the end of my life. I have, indeed before, had occasion to be present, and even to be a speaker, in that same noble area, the Piece-hall of this town; but then it was upon occasions which took place amidst the maddle of electioneering bustle and the din of political excitement. I confess, that it was a very pleasant and a very soothing contrast to be present in that same space, upon an occasion when all who are brought together seem to breathe the same atmosphere of good will, of harmony, and of love ; and I felt sure that no more precious and acceptable offering could arise to the skies than the hymn which came from so many thousands of artless youthful lips, and the homage that I hope ascended to the same quarter from hearts upon which the passions and vices of the world have as yet been able to infix no stain. But, gentlemen, glad as I was to be present at the assembly of young children this morning, and amply as I participated in all the emotions which that exhibition was calculated to convey, I feel I pay a debt of still more strict justice and obligation by coming this evening among the instructors and teachers of those children, — among those who not only teach the infant notes to join in the hymn of praise, but those whose higher and still nobler endeavour it is to instruct the youthful mind and to improve the youthful heart. Such, my friends — whether men or women — such is your praiseworthy and noble endeavour; and I have long felt convinced, both from what I have observed, and still more from what I have been able to collect and learn from others, that it is scarcely possible to overrate the real solid and practical good which is conferred upon our common country by its Sabbath school teachers. There may be those who come forward more prominently and more noisily in the service of their species, in the busy and tumultuous scenes in which my lot is cast. When I resort to the great metropolis of this empire, I see crowds of people, some of them plunged in the giddy round of dissipation and the frivolous routine of fashion, — some of them striving, one after another, upon the ladder of ambition, and all engrossed in an absorbing course, whether of pleasure or of business. I will not deny, that it is the bounden duty and proper vocation of many to mix in those scenes, to bear their part in the strife of the political arena, and endeavour to do what good they can to their country and to their kind, in the various walks of public and political life : but those aims and those labours, however necessary in themselves, however laudable when properly pursued and duly superintended, are but too often mixed with the promptings of selfishness and vanity, and with the desire of personal aggrandisement. But no such drawback seems to me to present itself when we consider the exertions of the common Sunday school teachers, when we consider those exertions which it is your habit and your pleasure soberly, and quietly, and unostentatiously to carry on in your several districts and neighbourhoods, very often unmarked by society at large, very often without meeting the praise of your fellows, sometimes even encountering their obloquy, sometimes provoking their ridicule; sometimes being questioned how you can be weak and foolish enough to take so much pains about what does not concern you, and about what does not profit you; about that which does not actually put any money in the purse, which does not bring any grist, as they say, to the mill, — and with no other incitement but the sense of duty which you feel, in your own consciences, and the experience of the good, which, day by day, week by week, and year by year, is manifesting itself around you; for you best know— you, the instructresses and instructors of the Sabbath schools, best know, both what amount of real and practical good they are calculated to effect in this country, — and I will say in this county, situated and circumstanced as it is, and especially in so busy a manufacturing neighbourhood as this; or, rather, you best can feel what a void, what a cruel loss would be felt, if by any sudden calamity your ministrations could be closed, or the Sabbath schools of this active district shut up and abandoned. I know it must be often irksome to you; I am willing to suppose that you will not have been influenced by that weak and unprincipled scoffing to which I have just alluded; I know that you will think, when the path of duty is plain before you, it is your duty to tread it. But I feel that very often it is no common sacrifice you are called upon to make. I know what a life of toil, of exertion, and of watchfulness must be the lot of many of you. I know that many of you have to labour the whole week long in your warehouses, at your counters, in your shops, in your mills, in your factories, and in your quarries; and I can well conceive, that when the seventh day comes, especially after you have given its due portion to the services of the sanctuary,— I well know what a temptation there must be before you, either to enjoy those beauties of nature, and those pleasant walks with which this neighbourhood so eminently abounds, or to spend more time in the family circle and by the family fireside, and thus to rest in comparative inactivity altogether. But you forego these claims; you are willing to make the seventh day also, — I will not say a day of toil, but a day at least where love is labour; for you feel what an awful thing it would be to see the infant and young population of these crowded districts growing up, themselves subjected to wearing and harassing toil, often debarred from the opportunities of education, often destitute of a father's care and a mother's love, exposed to all the temptations of evil association and bad companionship,—you know what a desolating and awful thing it would be if this youthful population should grow up without any knowledge of the duty they owe to their neighbour, without any instruction in the faith which is to make them wise unto salvation and bring them to their God; and when I looked at that interesting crowd before us to-day, of those who, though now small in stature and weak in strength, are yet to furnish the skill and sinews which are to continue the wondrous processes of British manufacturing ingenuity and enterprise, and who are to bequeath the riches of English industry and augment the glories of the British name, when you, their teachers, are silent in your graves, I could not help breathing a fervent aspiration in my heart that when the time shall come for them to emerge into manhood, and they shall meet the crosses and be exposed to the temptations of this weary and wicked world—when for instance the invitation of the drunkard shall be sounding in their ears, or when the call to dissipation shall be spreading all its allurements before them,—the recollections and impression of the Piece Hall at Halifax might come upon their minds, that the infant hymn they had raised in the days of their youth might yet ring freshly in their ears, and that they might determine to abide by the better inspiration of their youth which you did so much to keep straight and active in the path of duty, in the ways of virtue, and in conformity to the will of God. It does not become one such as I am to offer anything in the way of advice or suggestion to such a meeting as the present, especially as I am quite ignorant whether there is the least occasion for it. But in considering the subject of Sabbath schools, it sometimes comes to my mind, that whereas the young people are themselves exposed to a great deal of toil and hard work during the week, and necessarily must undergo a considerable degree of lassitude, some degree of caution should be observed, lest the pleasing ideas which I should always wish to see attached to the Sabbath might be interfered with, and that too much confinement, too much keeping within doors, too much of what is called commonplace school work, should not be exacted from them. I know that the circumstances of their position in life, I know that the circumstances of this district, render it absolutely imperative, render it an unspeakable blessing, that Sunday schools should exist, should be encouraged, and should be increased; and it is because I wish them well, and it is because I wish you well in the charge you have so nobly undertaken of them, that I came here to-night. But still, one and all, I should wish you to remember that the string ought not to be strained too tight, that a proper degree of rest, relaxation, and of innocent amusements appropriate to the Sabbath should not be interfered with, and that the young should be enabled to associate it with ideas of enjoyment, and of calm and peaceful happiness. In what follows, I feel sure you have no need of being admonished by me or by anybody else; but I should be very sorry if in Sunday school teaching there was any of that degree of harshness or of crossness which sometimes will occur even among the most meritorious professors of week-day education. Let nothing occur on the Sunday which shall not convey an idea of love, and be connected with thoughts of peace and pleasantness. There was another most agreeable feature in the meeting of this morning, and that was the number and variety of the different denominations which it brought together. I always think religious differences — though I believe, at least in our day, they are likely to be inevitable — are among the most unpleasant and distressing features of the times, and anything to promote religious sympathy, religious concord, and religious harmony, I hail, even independently of its own recommendation and merits, with added cordiality. I do not say anything to tempt you to undervalue the respective differences which you have severally been led conscientiously to adopt. I know how much that is valuable depends upon a strict and steadfast and undeviating compliance with our own inborn sense of truth. But separate opinions may have separate spheres of action, just as in the concerns of that delightful art, which I believe you must have largely practised, from the proof and evidence I heard of it this day — I mean the art of music: one voice is a bass, another is a tenor, and there are various other learned names for them, all proving that separate voices have their distinct and separate offices. When parties are called upon to sing a solo or a duo, they make a distinction of parts, but then there is nothing to prevent all those united voices joining in that common chorus of praise and adoration with which the hymn concludes; and in that way I wish you to maintain your separate differences. Maintain them where you are bound to do so, in your own consci ences, in your own chapels, in your own cottages, but not so as to refuse to join in that common hymn of praise and adoration which all people in this world are surely intended to send up together to their common Creator and their common Redeemer. Now I have only to renew the expression of the very sincere sympathy which I feel with your objects, the very unfeigned admiration I entertain of the zeal and activity and self-denying love with which you pursue them. I know that the common awards of fame are usually bestowed upon persons and pursuits I think far less deserving of them. They are often given, in the first place and principally, to reward the destroyers and desolators of mankind, — those who spread carnage through peaceful realms, and visit with slaughter unoffending tribes of our species. But, my friends, my sisters, and my brothers, if you will allow me to call you so, you may not have the votes of senators and of Parliaments bearing your names, they may not appear in newspapers or in gazettes, but still, trust me, your labour is not lost, your reward insures itself. It is written in the approving sense of your own consciences; it is written in the gratitude, and, still more, in the improvement of the rising generation who are springing up to life and strength, and I hope to usefulness and to virtue, around you; it is written, above all, in the records of those awards which are to fix our fate in eternity, for I need not remind you by whom it is said — " He that doeth this to the least of these little ones doeth it unto me." I can add nothing to such encouragements. I most gratefully thank you for the kind attention you have now bestowed upon me. I accept with pleasure the signs you gave that you received and did not reject the relationship which I claimed with you.

YORKSHIRE UNION OF MECHANICS' INSTITUTES.

Huddersfield, June 1846.

LADIES AND GENTLEMEN,

Having been promoted by you to the honours of the chair, I have, in the first instance, to return my thanks to you for the invitation and permission to fill it, and to express to you the very lively pleasure which it gives me to meet you upon so agreeable and auspicious an occasion as the present. This, indeed, is not the first time at which I have had the gratification of occupying a similar post at a meeting of the Yorkshire Union of Mechanics' Institutes. I think it is now two years ago since I discharged the same office at the anniversary meeting then held in Wakefield. Then, gentlemen, I occupied what might be termed a private position; I was not then connected as a representative with the large constituency of the Riding in which we are now met. Since that occasion, I hope you will allow me to say, that I feel I have been regularly and legitimately qualified to fill the office which I now hold. I wish I could consider myself qualified in all respects, for I fear, as often happens to the chairmen of public meetings, that I am perhaps less accurately acquainted with the subject matter of which I have to speak than almost any of those by whom I am surrounded. I have not been able, from want of opportunity, perhaps from want of proper industry, to make myself so well acquainted as I should have wished to have been with the various operations and transactions of the separate Mechanics' Institutions in this Riding and in this county; and, therefore, I can only hope that those who will have to follow me will be able, as, indeed, I am confident they will, to supply all the deficiencies which must necessarily be found in my method of discharging the duties of the place I now fill. I had not even the privilege of attending the meeting of this morning. Therefore your chairman feels himself in the scarcely dignified position of having but little to say to you about the proper business of the meeting. But I know enough of Mechanics' Institutes, — I know enough of the good they are calculated to effect, — I know enough of the good they have effected, — I know enough of the encouragement which has been given them in this county, — and nowhere, perhaps, in a more marked degree than in the town of Huddersfield, in which we are now met, — to be able to express my full sympathy in the success of the cause which has brought us together this evening, and to join my exhortation to all the others that will be addressed to you, to give to these institutions every encouragement and support in your power. It is a rule most properly laid down at these anniversary meetings, that topics of a nature which might excite difference of opinion, and which divide the community into separate demarcations — such as questions of political interest — should be excluded from our consideration; and I am sure, for one, I heartily wish that many of those who may be considered my political opponents may be numbered among those now present, in order to join their efforts with those of my political friends in promoting an object destined to secure the common good of all. There is, however, one matter which has much occupied public attention of late, to which I cannot help briefly adverting — not for the sake of considering its political bearing, not for the sake of eliciting any opinion respecting it from any person who may be now present — but only in so far as I think it is properly and naturally connected with the specific business of the evening. The subject to which I allude is the question of the Corn Laws. And why do I make mention of that? Because, without adverting more at length to what is now passing around us, I trust that if we are justified in considering that this large question is settled — that this great controversy is cleared off, and has left an open stage, I trust I am then justified in recalling to your recollection, that there may be other questions eminently deserving of your attention, lying beyond it, and that even this question of the food of the people ought not to absorb all the legitimate benevolence — all the manly effort which may be stirring among you. I am sure that I shall be the very last person to underrate the importance of that great subject to which I have thus briefly ventured to allude. But it must be confessed, that, important as it is, it primarily at least is a question which refers to our material wants — to the body's food — to the body's growth — to the body's being. Now, bear in mind that the body, though it is much, — though it is that without which there can be nothing else, yet still it is not all — it is not the most important — it is not the most enduring — it is not the most divine part of man's nature. We may be right in our opinion that a repeal of the Corn Laws would not only bring more wheat for the food of man, but that it would bring more oats for horses, more maize for cattle, more provender for pigs. Well, that would be enough for them — the body's food would be enough for them. But men who think and reason — men who speak and argue — men who can form themselves into societies, and can receive and impart instruction, and can enrol themselves as members of Mechanics' Institutes, know that they require more than the bread that groweth stale, and more than the meat that perisheth. What may not be effected by the physical skill and ingenuity of man? His lips may utter, and his ears may drink in, all the modulations of sound and of melody; his eye may dispose the most ingenious intricacies of the most delicate patterns, and regulate the assortments of the most striking and splendid colours; his hand may mould the breathing brass or the speaking marble; and, above all, his mind may apply the wisdom of the past for the instruction of the future; it may solve the highest questions of science and philosophy; it may unfold the countless mysteries, the peerless beauties of nature, or it may people time and space with the most radiant creations of the fancy. Well, then, after we have provided for the body its coarser, though indispensable nourishment, I hope that additional care and additional knowledge will be brought into play to provide for those higher requirements to which I have just adverted. When Leagues and Legislatures have done all that in them lies to provide the body's food, I hope you will feel that your next great object is more completely to educate the mind, more thoroughly to elevate the soul. We shall then expect Lord John Russell to write one of his pithy letters against the evils of ignorance, which are still more mischievous, and still more fatal, than those evils of destitution, of fever, and of mortality, which he so feelingly denounced. We shall expect Sir Robert Peel to bring in his Bills, and to carry them too, with the same stout will which has lately signalised him, for the introduction of a system for the general education of the people. And we shall expect our Cobdens and our Brights to do battle for free trade in slates and primers, for cheap arithmetic, cheap chemistry, cheap geography, cheap astronomy, for learning for the many, and literature for the millions. Now, among the undertakings and institutions which have been most successful in promoting the instruction and enlightenment of the mass of the people, Mechanics' Institutes have occupied a prominent and distinguished place. I believe it was a Yorkshireman, the late Dr. Birkbeck, who was the first pioneer in introducing Mechanics' Institutes; and I think it must be confessed that, in Yorkshire, these noble and praiseworthy institutions, to this day, have found a congenial soil. I find, from the official records which have been presented at the regular meeting of the union, that twenty-nine institutions in this county were, before this day, connected with the union; and that twenty of these institutions contained an aggregate of 5594 members. I find that twenty-three other institutions applied, and I am happy to say, what is better than applying, they have to-day been admitted into the Union.

These twenty-three institutes number 3440 members. The aggregate of the number of members of Mechanics' Institutes in Yorkshire, connected with the Union, now amounts to above 9000 persons. There is a further gratifying circumstance, that the increase of members has, in the short space of two years, been one-fourth. Comparing the number of members with the number of the gross population of the districts in which the institutions are founded, it appears that one in every fifty-four persons is a member of one of the Mechanics' Institutes, while in some of the smaller towns — I may mention Pateley bridge and Ackworth — one in every seventeen of the inhabitants is a member of a Mechanics' Institute. Why should the larger towns not take a lesson from their smaller contemporaries? Then I find that various methods are adopted in these institutions. One locality finds that one system suits its operations better, while another seems better suited to a different atmosphere. But one great benefit and advantage of this union, and of this annual gathering, is, that it admits the several members to compare notes with each other, — to find what has succeeded in one place, and what has failed in another, — what is attracting members in one district, and what is repelling them in another, — what tends, in one place, to give a serious and practical character to the operations of the institutes, while, in another, anything which may be looked upon as of a more frivolous or derogatory character may, in its turn, be avoided. I am happy to find that, in all these institutions, several schemes most advantageous and most profitable have been established. In some of them there are all the varieties, while in others one or two obtained a greater vogue. I find that, in thirty-eight institutions, there are libraries which have 38,000 volumes, with an issue, in one year, of 173,000 volumes, made to 7900 members. With respect to evening classes, they seem to me to be one of the most profitable, and one of the most unobjectionable modes of operation which these institutes can assume. One third of the members of the associated institutes are, in the evening classes, receiving instruction in the various branches of knowledge. Eighteen of the institutions have given 235 lectures during the past year; twenty others have given 150; and the whole thirty-eight institutions have given nearly four hundred lectures during that period. In some towns and cities there are young and kindred institutions which go under the names of "Youths' Guardian Societies,"

"Mutual Instruction Associations," and "Mutual Improvement Societies;" and I would respectfully advise the members of Mechanics' Institutions not to feel any jealousy or grudge of these kindred societies, if they should exist in any town, and should, on the first sight, be thought to detract from the apparent numbers of the Institute itself. Depend upon it, that in this, as in higher matters, all that are not against us are with us; all that are seeking the same object — that are seeking to refine and elevate the taste, the intellect, and the soul, are most useful adjuncts and allies to Mechanics' Institutes, whatever name they may bear. Then I think that the members of these Institutes have exercised much wise discretion in not confining their branches of occupation to the severer sciences — to the drier, if they are the loftier, branches of learning, but have included within their range the domain of the fine arts, and some of the more polite accomplishments. I find that in many of these institutes there are drawing classes. At Halifax, there is an Art-Union for the pupils of the drawing classes, which is thrown open to the town; and in Huddersfield and Leeds, Schools of Design have been established in connection with the Mechanics' Institutes. Now, I rejoice extremely that this should be the case; and I would hold out this example to general imitation, because it seems to me that the delightful arts of drawing and of painting, provided they do not withdraw those who pursue them from those occupations which are necessary for them to follow, are pursuits which not only contribute to enlarge and exalt the taste, but it seems to me that an improved and inventive facility of design must tend greatly to promote the special pursuits of which such districts and such towns as these are the theatre. Where is it so much called for to make yourselves instructed in all the witcheries of design and in all the wonders of colour, as for the use of those looms, the products of which must arrest the giddy caprice of fashion, and captivate the fastidious glance of beauty? Where is it so proper to elicit all the combinations and inventions of the fancy as in that town which is the mart of the fancy trade? I do not mean that you ought to attempt to transfer to your tweeds, to your lastings, to your cassimeres, to your waistcoats, and to your trousers, the matchless outlines of a Raphael, or the glowing tints of a Titian, any more than I should expect that lectures given on the art of poetry should turn out so many ready-made Miltons and

Shakspeares, or lectures on astronomy so many Newtons and Herschels. But I entertain the conviction that a sound knowledge and appreciation of the principles of science will make you appreciate more rightly the real force of truth and reason, and also that a sound knowledge and appreciation of art will tend to fix in your mind, and to bring out in the products of your hands, the indelible stamps of proportion and of beauty. Then I find that in some of the Institutes there are classes for acquiring a competent knowledge of modern languages: and this seems to me to be a pursuit highly desirable in this age, in this country, and in this district. Why, the carriers and agents in the highways of commerce are, in some sense, the citizens of every clime, and are free of every community; and why should not our young men be able to drive their bargains, whether it be for the fleeces of Spain or for the oils of Italy, in the harmonious and soft tongues of those regions? I do not know whether my excellent friend, your worthy President, Mr. Schwann, would expect me to apply the same epithets precisely to his native tongue, but I am sure you all must be alive to the importance of rivetting, as closely as possible, the ties between the people of this country and the great German family. I also observe that in other of the Institutes there are classes set apart for acquiring a knowledge of the principle and practice of singing; and this, I think, in its place, is a very good pursuit too. I believe that the West Riding of Yorkshire has long been famous for its warblers. You will recollect that it is said that

"The man that hath not music in his soul
Is fit for treasons, stratagems, and spoils."

And so I believe that to sing gaily, cheerily, and in tune from the heart, it is almost necessary to have a good conscience. The graver pursuits, the severer walks of knowledge, carry their own recommendation with them. They must recommend themselves to all intelligent and inquiring minds; and, believe me, those who have pursued them in earnest—those who have dived most deeply into them, find that they bring with them their own reward. I do not feel it necessary, in addition to what I have said, to guard myself against attaching to knowledge, to science, to art, to fancy, and to genius, any undue or exaggerated value; I know that good and acceptable as they all are, yet there are better things even than these — things more important for man's happiness, and for man's virtue. I know that all you can ever read, and all you can ever learn, must fall short of a good temper and a good conscience. By a good temper I mean such a temper as will make you willing workmen, kind husbands, and affectionate fathers; and I will add — for I learn with great pleasure that some of the institutes have adopted the valuable and powerful aid of female association and help, — such a temper as will make you considerate wives and conscientious mothers; and by a good conscience, I mean such a conscience as will make you and keep you good Christians and good citizens. Well, gentlemen, by the side and in comparison with such attributes and qualities as these, I willingly admit to you, that the loftiest soarings of the intellect, and the brightest imaginations of the fancy, are poor and valueless. But surely it is a very vulgar and a very stupid error, to neglect or to repel anything that is good, because there may be something better. We are not apt to refuse a shilling, because we should think it still better to have a sovereign. We know that a shilling added to a sovereign will make a guinea; and so will knowledge enhance even the true value of virtue; and knowledge, like the shilling, very often tends to make up the whole sum of man's real sovereign virtue. And so, Ladies and Gentlemen, whom I am happy to look upon as the combined friends, and patrons, and members of Mechanics' Institutes, I trust that you will add to your knowledge, virtue; and that, in fostering and extending the range of these institutions, you will do what in you lies to make the toiling, heaving, straining mass of the population—too likely to be led astray, — too likely to be corrupted by evil associations and bad companionship, if left without the softening and elevating influences of taste and knowledge, — a cultivated, an educated, and if so, all the more probably, a contented and a virtuous people.

BRADFORD MECHANICS' INSTITUTION.
October 6th, 1846.

LADIES AND GENTLEMEN,

I believe that it now becomes part of my pleasing duty to open the proceedings of this evening, and in doing so I cannot refrain from observing at the commencement that I believe, though I have in several instances been in the town of Bradford, upon occasions of political excitement and upon the eve of contested elections, yet that it has never fallen to my lot before to visit Bradford on what I may be allowed to call a purely social occasion. And I have felt, that considering what the importance of this town and district is, and the conspicuous place which it fills in the manufacturing history of our country, its being in fact the seat and capital of one of the principal branches of our manufactures, the worsted manufacture of the country, and its having exhibited, perhaps, a more striking and prodigious growth than any other town whatever within the limits of the kingdom,— having, as I am told, from the beginning of the century, when it scarcely amounted to 5000 inhabitants, now risen to the ample dimensions of 100,000,—and, remembering further that it has been my agreeable duty to attend in other towns in your neighbourhood, having been at Huddersfield, at Halifax, at Leeds, and at Wakefield, upon occasions not in any way connected with politics, — I did feel glad that the time was at last come when Bradford was no longer to be an exception to that rule. In a town circumstanced as this is, among all the toiling, struggling, panting hives of men, women, and children which it includes, where so much of time and thought must necessarily be engrossed by the strain of the daily task, and by the care for the daily meal, I do think it most desirable and most salutary to have some common neutral ground, restricted to no condition, limited to no class, sacred to no denomination, but where all alike equally, and at all times, can meet together, without any restraint save that of mutual self-respect — without any laws save those of good manners, for the salutary and noble purpose of acquiring in the first place useful information; in the next place, of gaining some proficiency in any elegant accomplishment; or, in the last place, of partaking in innocent recreation. I think that in a community so situated it is most desirable not only to furnish facilities for your becoming proficients in study, and in the acquisition of useful knowledge, but also to provide means of enlarging the sum of human cheerfulness and contentment. I am glad, therefore, that you should come to the Bradford Mechanics' Institute, that you should come to its libraries, that you should come to its lecture rooms. I wish that all those who feel so proper and honourable an ambition should come here at one time with the view of acquiring some knowledge of the wonderful workings of nature, such as they are developed to us by the processes of inquiry and by the conclusions of science. I am happy to find that some of your lectures are set apart to these high and ennobling pursuits. I am happy, above all, to find that one of your number, a gentleman connected officially with the highest duties of this town, I allude to your Rev. Vicar,* not only makes presents of his works to you, but is himself the writer of works worthy to be presented. I am glad that at other times you should come here to gain a competent knowledge of the history of bygone ages, not only as that history concerns itself with the details of wars, which have too often been both bloody and unfruitful, with the mere annals of courts, with the intrigues of statesmen, and with the policy of sovereigns who perhaps may be only aiming at their own personal aggrandisement, but of that history which penetrates into the deeper causes that enter inwardly into the life of nations, that decide the laws by which states flourish and by which states decay, that affect the real condition, the average happiness, the daily comfort of the great bulk of the people. I am glad that at other times you should come to make yourselves adequately instructed in what is called the study of biography, in the histories and fortunes of those more remarkable men who have been the lights and models of the ages in which they lived — not only of distinguished generals and mighty warriors, who, though we may regret the effects on human happiness which have too frequently resulted from the bare pursuit of military glory, yet still in the details of their individual lives may often furnish very high and inspiriting lessons of difficulties subdued and hardships encountered, — but that you should augment your knowledge of those who have been the more real benefactors of the ages in which they lived, and who are therefore at least as fully entitled to the gratitude of nations, while they may divide with the others their admiration ; — I mean the inventors of useful arts, the discoverers of lofty truths, the martyrs to the sense of right and to the call of duty. And it is pleasing to think that our own times will be able to furnish many splendid contributions to the list of Worthies which I have thus characterised as proper subjects for Biography to concern herself with, and that she will be able to hand down to the latest posterity, together with the unconquered sword of Wellington, the equally enduring record of names such as that, for instance, of Thomas Clarkson, the man who

* The Rev. Mr. Scoresby.

gave the first impulse to the movement which led to the final extinction of the African slave trade, over whose honoured, but not immature grave, all who are best and most philanthropic in the land are now joining together in respectful sympathy. Well, then, I wish that those who feel the due ambition should come to your lectures and to your libraries, to advance and to improve themselves by such studies as those of history and biography; but I think, also, that after the tear and wear of daily labour in your workshops and factories, it would be very captious to object to a man, at the close of a well-spent day, if he felt disinclined at the time to give his attention to any of those severer pursuits, relaxing his mind either with the perusal of good poetry or of graceful fiction. With respect to poetry, I need hardly tell you that, in its proper sphere, lessons as thrilling and as exalting may be derived from the pen of gifted poets as from the most prosaic writings to which we could turn our attention; and, perhaps you will allow me to say, upon this head, at least, that your library, which seems upon the whole to be very well and prudently selected, hardly contains as yet such an assortment of good poets as I think ought to be found in it. And with respect to fiction too, though I would not recommend it as giving the same healthy tone and nourishment to the mind as other more practical pursuits, yet I am pleased to think, especially in later times, that writers of fiction have treated it both with so much refinement and so much enlargement of view, that lessons may be derived from the pages of the best writers of fiction, be they male or female, scarcely inferior to what can be derived from the study of facts. But then, ladies and gentlemen, are you ever too tired even to attend to reading of any sort, or have you no fancy, after a hard day's work, to take up the pages of any book? Well, then, occasionally, I certainly am not sorry to find that you have been in the habit, in this large apartment, of seeking further relaxation in good music and in occasional concerts. Still I know that good concerts and good music cannot be had without some considerable cost, and I think it would not be difficult to devise even less expensive pleasures with which occasionally to vary the long evenings of the winter. Now, why should not any of you, accustomed to come here after a day's work, meeting in the reading room or the library, occasionally prevail upon some one of your number who may be a good reader, — and I am sure such are likely to be found among you — to read from one valuable work or other; or even why could you not enlist some one amongst those who are looked up to as moving in the more opulent classes amongst you, who would be good enough to give his time for such a purpose, and to read to any that may be gathered together in the evening, one of the best plays of Shakspeare, or a piece of Milton's Paradise Lost? And if you should find that the taste grows upon you, you might even take up Pope's Homer's Iliad. However, I leave all that to your own taste and discretion. Respecting those topics which relate more to the accomplishments and to the fine arts, I think it is very gratifying to find that you have established a school for drawing, and that it excites considerable interest among you. I hope you will carry that delightful pursuit still farther; and besides, it cannot be looked upon as a mere idle accomplishment, or as a mere delightful recreation — it will even stand the test of this utilitarian age. This town is largely engaged in manufactures. As I have said, it is busied with one of the principal branches of the manufactures of this country, and it is a branch of those manufactures in which the art of making suitable patterns and designs must find a place. Now, it is a well-known fact that in many respects the manufactures of this country defy all competition, and that in the adaptation of our machinery and in the intelligence of our operatives we are not afraid to confront the whole of the Old world and the New. But it is not less acknowledged by those who take an impartial view on such subjects, that we are inferior to many nations on the Continent as yet in the arts of design and colour, and that we have not arrived quite at that happy delicacy in making out those beautiful combinations in patterns at which some of our neighbours, especially the French, have arrived. Now, I believe there is nothing in the natural composition or genius of Englishmen which unfits them from excelling here as well as in other respects; but they have not yet made it part of their practical, positive business to attend to it; and with this view schools for drawing are most eminently useful. It may be that in drawing schools, where you have models put before you of the human form and other objects of that sort, you cannot see at first sight of what good they can be to you in making out a pretty and delicate pattern; but depend upon it that the eye which has been trained to all the true doctrines of proportion and beauty, will attain comparative excellence in every branch of labour to which it applies itself. And I do most earnestly hope that not only the working classes, the operative men, those who have to carry on the handiwork of the manufacturers, will attend to this suggestion, but that the great employers of labour will take it into their earnest consideration, too. I hope on all accounts that they will give an enlightened and liberal support to the general purposes of this institution. I feel it to be eminently their duty, but not more their duty than their interest, to take every means of surrounding themselves with an orderly, a refined, an intellectual, and an educated population, and I believe they will find this to be the case in every respect. It will return upon them in a thousand ways however little immediately concerned the subject-matter of the studies may appear with the daily business with which they are connected; but as the poet Pope, whom I have once mentioned before, and whom I may specify, perhaps not as the first, perhaps not as the greatest, but as the most perfect of our poets, says—

"Thus God and Nature link'd the gen'ral frame,
And bade self-love and social be the same."

by promoting the good of others, you are sure in the end to promote your own; and so upon the most sordid calculations of interest, upon what concerns your pockets, you may depend upon it, that if in the long run the patterns and manufactures of other countries exhibit a decided superiority over your own, you will lose your hold of the market of the world. And, therefore, besides encouraging good order, besides encouraging general knowledge, besides encouraging useful information amongst those by whom you are surrounded, also promote that taste for beauty, that true conception of the loveliness of nature of which art is but another embodiment, and you will find it the best means, not only of advancing and elevating the population in which you live, but of rendering yourselves superior to all the competition of the world's rivalry. I am glad with this view to find that it is in the contemplation of the committee to found, I believe, a new condition of admission, by which, if a person subscribe a guinea a year to the funds of this Institution, he shall not only be entitled to share in all its privileges and advantages himself, but shall have the privilege of introducing two pupils gratuitously to all its benefits. And most gratified I should be to learn that the great manufacturers and employers of labour in Bradford avail themselves of this condition not only to associate themselves with this Institution, which I think would reflect such just credit upon them, but to give the means to those least able to afford it, of reaping the benefit which it holds out to its members. I am glad, also, to find another contemplated condition, which I think is conceived in the true spirit of Yorkshire liberality and hospitality, — that condition is, that when any member of any other Mechanics' Institution in the West Riding of Yorkshire shall be resident for a time within this town, he shall be entitled to free admission to the benefits of this Institution. I think this is an admirable rule, calculated not only to extend the benefits of your Institution, but to promote the advantages of communication and feelings of good fellowship among all those who are brought together by kindred tastes and by kindred pursuits. It would be in vain for me to dissemble, ladies and gentlemen, now that I have offered the few practical remarks which have occurred to me — it would be in vain for me to dissemble what interest I feel in all that concerns the real interests, and what pride I take in all that advances the real character of the inhabitants of this Riding. This important district comprises a vast number of large towns and communities which are themselves the seats and centres of kindred and analogous, though, I believe, in many respects, of somewhat different branches of manufacture. Well, what I want you to do is, not to vie with each other alone in the skill of your handicraft, or in the ingenuity of your machinery, or in the accumulation of your capital, but in the nobler growth of the mind, the intellect, and the character. Be careful to show that upon this generous and splendid field of competition, while you do not grudge being outstripped by any other town, you will not be content yourselves, if there be any danger, to remain the hindmost. You are now, most of you, and have been for some time, busily employed in connecting your several towns with each other by means of railways. Well, be equally careful to speed the intercourse of the mind as well as of the body. Do not let your "West Riding Unions" be confined merely to the railway world, but let them include in your care and in your liberality the Union of the West Riding Mechanics' Institutes, and all other institutions devoted to the like noble and improving purposes. Cut your first sod in the dense crust which has too long overlaid the genial capacities of the soil beneath — open the waste lands of selfishness, of ignorance, of prejudice, and of error, in order that you may call forth the full development of mental progress and moral culture; and let the free communication of knowledge, and the improving intercourse of thought, ply incessantly along those new highways which, in their advancing progress, are to bring together the wants and the attainments of the united human family.

MANCHESTER ATHENÆUM.
October, 1846.

I trust I shall be believed, when I say I appreciate my situation. Whatever may be the incidents of distinction, or responsibility, with which I am elsewhere invested—honoured as I am by the choice of no mean Constituency on the other side of the hills which bound your prospects—permitted as I am to bear a part in the highest councils of the State—I can in all truth assure you, that I find something very new, fresh, and large in the honour of being called upon to preside at this annual jubilee of the Manchester Athenæum. The sense of honour, and let me add with as much truth, of difficulty also, is certainly not lessened, when I call those to mind who have preceded me in the same post, upon these brilliant occasions. The last echoes of this assembly, which I now feel it is a hardihood in me to rouse again, answered to the accents, deep, gentle, and earnest as his own spirit, of Mr. Serjeant Talfourd—why, there is something in the very name of an Athenæum which bespeaks it to be a fitting theatre for all the utterances of the bard of *Ion* and the *Athenian* captive. Next before him, I well know that your souls must have thrilled under the spell of so potent a magician as Mr. D'israeli; even in the very hottest conflicts of party, from which we are here happily sheltered, I think it was impossible even for his most exposed victim to have been blind to the point, the brilliancy, the genius, which played about the wounds they made—but here, on this gorgeous stage, amidst this apt and congenial auditory, on the themes so familiar to him of literature, of art, of imagination, I, who could only read in cold print what he said, without all the kindling accessories of time and place, can yet easily believe how the admiration, which could not be withheld even on the barren ground of political controversy, must have here been heightened almost into enchantment. And it was at the first, I believe, of these assemblies, the first at least held upon this scale of size and splendour, that its chair was filled—better it can never again be filled—by Charles Dickens—that bright and genial nature, the master of our sunniest smiles and our most unselfish tears, whom, as it is impossible to read without the most ready and pliant sympathy, it is impossible to know (I at least have found it so) without a depth of respect, and a warmth of affection, which a singular union of rare qualities alike command. I have made it my business, too, to look at what they said when they were here; but this, while it certainly has ministered very highly to my gratification, has also only added to my embarrassment; for it would indeed be an endeavour irksome to you, and hopeless for me, to revive in feebler expression, and fainter colouring, what was pourtrayed by them with so much richness and exuberance. I therefore feel that at this time of day, and above all in this place, it would be an impertinence in me to inculcate that learning in any community will not prove "a dangerous thing"—that commerce, which has formed, and which now ennobles a community like this, is the natural ally of literature and art—that the tastes which may be here encouraged, the habits which may be here fostered, are those which give a grace and glory to the lives and characters of men. Yes, I do rejoice with the most gifted and ardent of those who have preceded me, of those who now surround me, — I do rejoice over the impulses and associations which are impressed upon the times we live in, and which institutions like this, and assemblies like these, serve to rivet and transmit; I rejoice that English commerce is rising up to the height of its position, and feeling the real dignity of its calling; but this the Tuscan, this the Genoese, this the Venetian did; the worthies of our English commerce are content to be merchants, without being princes; if we have Medicis, they are not intent on seeking alliances with the thrones of Europe; their best aim will be now to raise to the same level of knowledge, of happiness, of virtue, the whole body of the people. I rejoice that here, in Manchester, beyond all dispute the first city in the ancient or modern world for manufacturing enterprise and mechanical skill, you have not been content with that display of wealth which jostles in your streets and is piled in your warehouses; you do not think it enough to raise factories tier upon tier, and magazines that will accommodate the traffic of the world, but you have thought it part of your proper business, too, to build and to set apart a haunt for innocent enjoyment, for useful instruction, for graceful accomplishment, for lofty thought, the shrine of Pallas Athene in a Christian land. May this long be the resort, together with those kindred and neighbouring institutions, which this does not aim to eclipse or overlay, but to encourage and excite, where all who are engaged in the business and the labours of this unparalleled hive of industry may find rest for their flagging spirits, a neutral ground for their manifold differences, invigorating food for their reason, and an impulse, onward and upward, to all the higher tendencies of our nature. I am glad to perceive that, as the benefits of the establishment are confined to no condition, no class, no denomination, so they are not exclusively appropriated even to one sex. Women have always played an important, perhaps not uniformly a beneficial part in this world's history. I believe as civilisation advances, they will play both a more recognised and a more elevated part than they have ever yet done; and I trust that among the many currents upon which the restless activity of our age is eddying along, a prominent one will be devoted to making female education sound, substantial, and enlightened; all it ought to be for training those who themselves must in any case be the real trainers, as they may be the best trainers, of our citizens and our workmen. From all I can gather, the wholesome effects of your association have, by no means, been confined to its own walls or its own operations; it not only walks its own round, but is suggestive of many kindred processes; or, if I may borrow an illustration from one of the disputed problems of the upper skies, in its career of light and progress, it throws off from itself separate bodies, which harden into distinct masses, and glow with independent lustre. Has it not been very much under the impulse of ideas struck out and caught up here, in your lecture rooms, in your social gatherings, in the more earnest friction of your discussions, by the agency mainly of your members, your officers, your founders, that the public parks, which have added so much, both of material and of real beauty to your great city, that the public baths and wash-houses, which have still deeper effects than on the mere linen and the skin, that the attention given to sanitary regulations of every description, have owed their rise? Can you look to other sources for industrial schools, for the weekly half-holiday in warehouses, for the early closing of shops?

You will perceive that I have not refrained from some of those obvious topics in connection with the institution, which the part assigned to me of opening the proceedings of the night necessarily almost imposed upon me. Let me turn for a little time from the institution to yourselves,—you who constitute it, who are its essence and its life. I perceive that one of the orators by whose eloquence you have heretofore been so much delighted, addressing himself to the youth of Manchester before him, told them with emphasis to aspire. Far be it from me to tell them otherwise; all who feel within them the sacred flame, who are strung for the high endeavour, who have girded themselves for the immortal race, I would address in the same terms, even the terms of the great moralist poet, Dr. Johnson:—

"Proceed, illustrious youth,
And virtue guard thee to the throne of Truth!
Let all thy soul indulge the generous heat,
Till captive Science yield her last retreat;
Let Reason guide thee with her brightest ray,
And pour on misty Doubt resistless day!"

It is, indeed, by such means, by patient inquiry, by diligent study, by humble-minded searching after truth, that all real knowledge is to be wooed by man, equally removed from the shallow presumption which sets up its own speculations and sophistries in the place of a conscientious reason and a disciplined faith, and from the blind bigotry which bawls down fair argument, decides against proof, and condemns without hearing. But I was saying that I did not wish, I could not wish, to damp or discountenance the purpose of your young men to aspire; for well I know that genius is the property of no condition, the apanage of no class of men: it will often be seen to rise, like the Goddess of old, out of the ocean billow, from those surfaces of society where you would least expect to find it, break through all the surrounding uniformity, and shed sudden radiance round the new horizon. But, while I am ready to track its shining course, and bask in its genial warmth, in whatever orbit it may be moving, I would yet venture to remind you that there is something more admirable than genius, and that is virtue; there is something more valuable than success, and that is duty. The hope of succeeding in the world, and of playing a shining part, may sometimes operate powerfully as an incentive, but it is too apt to engross both the efforts and the admiration of mankind. I was struck with the import of an expression I once heard from a friend, though you will at once perceive that it is not to be understood quite in its literal acceptation: the expression was, that Heaven was made for those who had failed in the world. Now, all sorts of unbecoming and unamiable feelings may undoubtedly accompany and embitter failure, just as every bright and blessed quality of the heart and mind may enhance and adorn success; but to aim at success, to meet with failure, and not to grudge it, to be outstripped by a rival and yet

> "To hear
> A rival's praises with unwounded ear,"

this is an effort and a triumph besides which all the ordinary successes of life are mean and trivial. Success, after all, in nearly every walk of life, from the aspiring statesman to the ambitious parish beadle, unless very carefully watched, very anxiously chastened, is apt to be made up of very coarse, obtrusive, vulgar ingredients, certainly not of heavenly temperament; while there is hardly a grace of character, a spring of self-reliance, an element of progress, with which failure, not caused by our own acts, and sustained with an even and brave spirit, may not ally itself. Depend upon it, in a great many instances, the world does not discover, does not recognise its best; there are diamonds in Golconda more precious than any, the Pitt, or the Pigott, or the Kohinoor, which ever blazed in the diadem of sovereigns; there are pearls in unopened shells more lustrous than any that ever shone upon the neck of beauty; the ages as they pass have known their Homer, their Raphael, their Newton, their Shakspeare; but there are prodigalities among the human creation as well as among all besides, that have never yet been fathomed; yet there has never been any thing which, except by its own fault, has been lost or thrown away. Which is the material point,—to be Raphael or Shakspeare, or only to be thought a transcendant poet, or an unequalled painter; to have conceived in the inmost soul the lineaments of the Holy Mother and Divine Babe, the idea of *Lear* on the heath, or *Macbeth* at the banquet, or to have would-be amateurs commending the picture, and crowded audiences shouting bravo in the pit? Only impress upon your minds this great truth — and bear it about with you both to your daily task and to your evening leisure, both to the privacy of your homes, and to your social musters, that it matters comparatively little what we may seem to be — it even matters proportionately little what we may do: what we are matters every thing; what we may seem, is subject to a thousand accidents and misapprehensions; what we may do, is under the control of circumstances; what we are, is entirely under our own. We may be all we should be; and no matter how humble the situation may be of any one among you, no matter how obscure the business which engrosses every precious hour, how insignificant the whole life's drudgery, still in that obscure and unenvied situation, amidst that wearing and numbing drudgery, you may mould for yourselves the qualities, you may build up for yourselves the character which princes, if they knew it, would trust, which multitudes, if they could discern it, would adore. I know that in venturing to speak upon these high topics of morality and conduct, with lips scarcely authorised, I run the risk of imperfect explanation, as well as of much misconstruction. I know it is thought that addresses delivered on such occasions are rather apt to minister too much to the pride of man — to undue adulation of the intellect. I disclaim such tendencies; when I say you may be all you should be, I do not mean to exclude from the method those aids and sanctions which are too high to be here dwelt upon, and no one feels more convinced that reason as well as Christianity makes humility almost its most prominent grace. Who would not be humble who felt, as he ought, the loveliness of virtue, and the magnificence of knowledge? I should like to ask the men who have just added another planet to our system, or, as has been beautifully said, on an earlier occasion, "who lent the lyre of heaven another string," whether their spirit does not recoil with modest awe, instead of swelling with self-sufficient pride, before the secrets of that space into which they have been permitted to throw a more far-seeing gaze than any of their fellows; and when the time shall come which to our enlarged and perfected vision shall unfold the whole bright mechanism of stars, and suns, and systems, shall we not find in the laws which fix their stations, or which guide their mazes, fresh reasons to be reverent, acquiescent, and lowly? It is time, however, for me to come down from the clouds, and indeed from everything else; I could hardly, however, have lighted on a more radiant resting-place on this earth than the present assembly. I only hope that all those who have partaken in its excitements will not merely carry away the transitory emotions to which it may easily give birth, but a settled determination, followed up by a corresponding practice, to give fair play and full scope to all the best and highest purposes of which the Institution is capable; they must be attained by associated effort, but you will hardly fail to remark, at least it is generally the case in institutions of this character, how very much of the work is done by a very few out of the whole number. Now, what we want is more of individual energy in the whole body; each of you make the work his own; and let no member of the Manchester Athenæum think that he has done his duty without having done something, according to his opportunities, to give encouragement, efficacy, and credit to an establishment he ought to be so proud to serve. On my own part I have only further to say, that if, when the gay glitter of the scene has passed away,—when the strains of music are hushed, and silence has fallen on the voice of the speaker,—any one of you, in the stillness of the quiet home, or amid the clang of the daily occupation, shall have derived a single encouragement to ennobling reflections or to worthy pursuits,—still more if any, under the sting of disappointment, or a sense of the world's coldness and alienation, shall have been reminded how little it really signifies, and that failure is one of the appointed accesses to Heaven, —if any word that has fallen from me shall have contributed to such encouragement or such alleviation, I shall then feel that I have not come to Manchester quite in vain.

SHEFFIELD ATHENÆUM.
September, 1847.

MY LORDS, LADIES, AND GENTLEMEN,

I could not resist the gratification, when it was proposed to me, of attending the meeting of this evening, brought together for the purpose of promoting the interests of the Sheffield Athenæum and Mechanics' Institution, and of encouraging its friends in the good work they have undertaken. I feel, indeed, that having now been called upon to attend some half-dozen meetings within this Riding, for the same purpose and with the same objects, that it would be quite useless for me to endeavour to bring any new illustration, or to offer any new suggestion, even upon a subject so important and interesting as that which engages our attention. You do well, ladies and gentlemen, to promote the objects of such an Institution as that which has now been founded for thirteen years within your town; and to which, I trust, a fresh impulse and encouragement have been given this day by the ceremony of the morning, in laying a first stone for a new and extensive building under the happy auspices by which you are distinguished upon the present occasion. I hope that the building is destined largely to extend the advantages which have already been derived from the establishment of a Mechanics' Institution within your town. I hope it is destined to associate with it several kindred objects, connected with the education generally of the youthful classes, and the promotion of a taste for the Fine Arts, which I can assure you will be found one of the most useful auxiliaries to the peculiar pursuits of this place, as well as highly conducive to the general improvement and elevation of all who can participate in those benefits. I am not, necessarily, intimately well acquainted with the peculiar processes and objects to which the attention of the Members of the Sheffield Mechanics' Institution has of late been directed. I think it is always desirable that the pursuits and studies should not be confined to any one branch of acquirement, inasmuch as the same food does not suit all palates, nor the same food at all times suit the same palates. I certainly hope that your foremost attention, and your most anxious patronage, will always be directed to those studies and objects which are most important for advancing the real, moral, political, and social improvement of your population—which tend to make the mind rational, sober, and manly, and which most fit them for battling in that great conflict of existence in which we must all bear a part, and enlisting under the banner of progress which is unfurled above us. But with those more serious, and solemn, and business-like pursuits, which ought to occupy your foremost attention, I think the promoters of this Institution have done well to mix some attention to the lighter walks of elegant accomplishments and polite literature, and to the cultivation of a taste for art, poetry, or music, which tend so much not only to relax, but to refine the human mind. While I recommend those who are inclined to such studies, to give their foremost attention to the severer walks of history and philosophy, I do not wish to exclude the graceful pages of poetry and fiction, and I will borrow an illustration from those pages, of the truth which I think worthy to be impressed upon your minds. Those of you who have had the opportunity of consulting the old legends of classical mythology, are aware that among the fancied deities with which they peopled the world, there was one who was more especially regarded as the God of labour, and of handicraft, Vulcan by name, who was always represented as being employed in huge smithies and workshops, hammering at heavy anvils, and blowing vast bellows, heating vast furnaces, and begrimed with soot and dirt. Well, for this hard working and swarthy-looking divinity, they wished to pick out a wife. And they did not select for him a mere drab—not a person, taken herself from the scullery or kitchen-dresser; but they chose for him Venus, the Goddess of love and beauty. Now, ladies and gentlemen, pick out for me the moral of this tale, for I believe that nothing ever was invented,—certainly nothing by the polished and brilliant imagination of the Grecian intellect, which has not its own meaning, and its moral. I have no doubt that all the legends of our own country—that the one even of your own neighbourhood, the Dragon of Wantley itself has its appropriate allegory and meaning, if we only knew how to find them out. But what is the special meaning of the marriage of Vulcan with Venus—of the hard-working artificer with the laughter-loving queen—of labour with beauty? What is it but this, that even in a busy hive of industry and toil like this, even here, upon a spot which is in many respects no inapt representative of the fabled workshop of Vulcan, even here, amid the clang of anvils, the noise of furnaces, and the sputtering of forges—even here, amid stunning sounds, and sooty blackness, the mind—the untrammelled mind—may go forth, may pierce the dim atmosphere which is poised all around us, may wing its way to the freer air and purer light which dwell beyond, and may ally itself with all that is most fair, genial, and lovely in creation. So, gentlemen, I say, your labour, your downright, hard, swarthy labour may make itself the companion, the helpmate, and the husband of beauty—of physical beauty, as I have reason to believe, from the inspection which I am able even now to command, and I have no doubt that a more intimate acquaintance with your wives, sisters, and daughters, would enable me to prove that I was not here wrong in my illustration:—but besides this beauty, I say, your labour may ally itself with intellectual beauty—the beauty which is connected with the play of fancy, with the achievements of art, and with the creations of genius; beauty, such as painting fixes upon the glowing canvass, such as the sculptor embodies in the breathing marble, such as architecture developes in her stately and harmonious proportions, such as music dresses with the enchantment of sound. Now it is to the perception and cultivation of the beautiful in these departments that I look upon your Schools of Design, and your concerts, and many of the lectures which you hear from able and gifted men, as intended to be subservient; and I strongly advise the members of this Mechanics' Institution to show a discriminating and generous support of these tasteful and humanizing pursuits. Above all, I advise you to cultivate a love of reading—that which makes you almost independent of any other aids and appliances, and puts, with very moderate help, the whole domain of philosophy, history, and poetry, within your individual command. Why, gentlemen, a man is almost above the world, who possesses two books. I do not mean to put the two books which I am about to mention upon the same level, far from it, nor am I wishing to intimate to you that two books are sufficient for your study and perusal. I am only mentioning them as representatives of what is most excellent, though different in degree. But I say that a man is almost above the world who possesses his Bible and his Shakspeare — his Shakspeare for his leisure — his Bible for all time. I said some time ago, that labour, even the labour of this district, may unite itself with intellectual beauty. But there is a beauty of a still higher order with which I feel even more assured it is still more open to it to unite itself: I mean with moral beauty — the beauty connected with the affections, the conscience, the heart, and the life. It is indeed most true that in the very busiest and darkest of your workshops — in the most wearying and monotonous tasks of your daily drudgery, as also in the very humblest of your own homes — by the very smallest of your fireplaces — one and each of you, in the zealous and cheerful discharge of the daily duty — in respect for the just rights and in consideration for the feelings of others — in the spirit of meekness, and in the thousand charities and kindnesses of social and domestic intercourse, — one and each of you may attain to and exhibit that moral beauty of which I have spoken — that beauty which is beyond all others in degree, because, when it is attained to, it is the perfection of man's nature here below, and is the most faithful reflection of the will and image of his Creator. And thus, ladies and gentlemen, I close my explanation of the marriage of Vulcan with Venus — of Labour with Beauty, and with it I close the remarks which I have risen to offer you this evening. It has been a real pleasure to me to meet you here. I feel that this is neither the time nor the place fitting for me to enter upon any topics connected with local circumstances which are not properly connected with the business or occasion of our meeting. I have spoken of a just regard for the rights of others, and I feel quite disposed to believe that all who come within these walls are always willing to be actuated by a spirit of harmony and by a just regard to the rights and privileges of others. I have told you that labour — your labour — the labour of this district — may be most properly mated with beauty, but labour certainly loses its dignity and value if it is divorced from liberty. And it is by the aid of this and similar institutions — it is by the honest and genial influence which they have a tendency to spread around them, that I trust the intelligence and conscience of the times in which we live may be so fostered and so united, that every form and kind of tyranny may be effectually put down and banished;—the tyranny of opinion, the tyranny of classes; the tyranny of the few, the tyranny of the many. And it is by the salutary control which an instructed and enlightened public will be competent to exercise over the conduct and march of affairs that you will be best able to guard yourselves, on the one hand, against undue and vexatious interference on the part of governments and rulers, and on the other hand against the abuses and neglect of local and individual interests; and that you will be able to attain that which ought to be the true aim of a nation's management, the pursuit of the best ends by the most efficient methods.

YORKSHIRE UNION OF MECHANICS' INSTITUTES.
Hull, June, 1848.

LADIES AND GENTLEMEN,

I have to assure you that it is with very great pleasure that I find myself associated with you on this occasion. Though I am not so able as are many of those by whom I am surrounded to give you an account of the recent proceedings of the Yorkshire Union of Mechanics' Institutions; though I am still less competent, from any actual experience, to enter into the concerns of the Athenæum of Hull; yet I trust that you will consider that I am not out of place on this occasion. For I will beg to remind my East Riding friends among you, that I have the honour to be an office-holder in this riding. But we do not, on this occasion, consider ourselves to be limited by the boundaries of ridings, or even of counties; and it is with no small pleasure that I see, upon this occasion, associated with us, my friend the Earl of Yarborough, and any coadjutors he may have brought with him from the county of Lincoln. I know that he and his tenantry, to say the very least, are prepared to compete with the whole world in the science and the practice of farming; and it is gratifying to find that there is no field of improvement, no branch of progress, in which they are not willing to lend a helping hand. It was said of old, by the great French king, when he put his grandson upon the throne of Spain, that there were thenceforth to be no Pyrenees; so we, when any object of rational import, or any opportunity of social intercourse is to be imparted, may henceforth say, "There shall be no Humber." Now, with respect to this special occasion which has brought us together, I always must feel, that a person who wishes to recommend any institution or undertaking to general support and acceptance, ought to be careful lest he should seem unadvisedly to exaggerate its pretensions, or to put them in a false light. So I do not, on this occasion, — though I think the advantages to be derived from Mechanics' Institutes, and other similar enterprises, are very great and very various, — yet I do not affect to place them upon the same level as the observance of industry and honesty in the course of business; or, in the daily habit of our life, as the cultivation of domestic virtues, or household charities, or the all-comprehensive relations which subsist between man and his Creator. I should also think that person a very injudicious friend to Mechanics' Institutes who should pretend that, in your reading-rooms and lecture-rooms, the means were afforded of turning out your members as finished scholars, or ready-made philosophers, or of conferring those distinctions which must always be the reward of the midnight oil of the student, or the life-long researches of the experimentalist. But, if it be the object how to raise the toiling masses of our countrymen above the range of sordid cares and low desires — to enliven the weary toil and drudgery of life with the countless graces of literature, and the sparkling play of fancy, — to clothe the lessons of duty and of prudence in the most instructive as well as the most inviting forms, — to throw open to eyes, dull and bleared with the irksome monotony of their daily task-work, the rich resources and bountiful prodigalities of nature, — to dignify the present with the lessons of the past and the visions of the future, — to make the artisans of our crowded workshops and the inhabitants of our most sequestered villages alive to all that is going on in the big universe around them, and, amidst all the startling and repelling distinctions of our country, to place all upon the equal domain of intellect and of genius; — if these objects — and they are neither slight nor trivial — are worthy of acceptance and approval, I think that they can be satisfactorily attained by the means which Mechanics' Institutes place at your disposal; and it is upon grounds like these that I urge you to tender them your encouragement and support. Then, if

Mechanics' Institutes are entitled to general favour, — if institutions such as the Athenæum and the Mechanics' Institute of this place are a credit and an ornament to the district in which they are placed, it does not require any expression of argument to prove to you that such an institution as the Yorkshire Union of Mechanics' Institutes must have a tendency to increase and diffuse the practical benefits for which the separate branches are designed; for it is the means of spreading, on every side, the most useful information, — of pointing out the best models, — of conducting to what are the most praiseworthy objects, and the most ready means of successfully prosecuting them. It enables the inhabitants of our smaller manufacturing villages to know what has been successfully effected in the great commercial emporiums of Sheffield and Leeds; it enables the farmers and yeomen of the Wolds to know what is achieved under the graceful towers of Beverley or around the crowded quays of Hull. I believe I am correct in the assertion that Yorkshire alone — that the district comprised in the Yorkshire Union of Mechanics' Institutes, contains a greater number of those institutions than any other, with respect to its area and population, in the whole kingdom. I find that the total number of Mechanics' Institutions in the Yorkshire Union is 86, and the aggregate number of members 15,860. As might be expected, these institutions present to us a variety of features.

I think it almost unnecessary to explain the advantages of good lectures; but I may state that the accession of Howden to the Union is attributable to Mr. Child's lectures in that place. In the same manner, the exertions of Mr. Dunning have led to the accession of Market Weighton. I believe that the East Riding sub-union, in the most public-spirited manner, has seen the advantages of this method of providing instruction and amusement, and has hired a lecturer of its own. I am informed that in consequence of the facility and arrangements of the Yorkshire Union, the sum of 113*l*. has been saved by the respective institutions of which it is composed, by uniting in the engagement of well-qualified public lecturers, above what would have been paid by the separate institutions had they all separately engaged those lecturers. As might be expected, different modes of attraction have been resorted to. At Leeds, I believe, no money whatever is taken at the door for the lectures, but they find that good lectures so increase the members, that they have no need to resort to extraneous means of support. I believe I may congratulate this institution — at whose special invitation we are met in this place — upon mixing wholesome recreation with the severer studies of literature. The Hull Athenæum has a cricket club of its own. At Saddleworth, the ladies enter so much into the spirit of the institution that, I am informed, they write essays which are read by their friends, the members of the institute. Leeds and Wakefield add to the attractions of the library and the lecture-room others of the Muses, and give monthly concerts. Most important benefits have been found in some places to result from the classes formed for adults, who are immersed in various occupations during the entire day, but meet together in the evening for the acquisition of those elements of education which they have not, perhaps, had the opportunity of acquiring in their youth. In this way at Huddersfield, an institution has met with much success, and working men may command great facilities for education, for sixpence a fortnight. I believe at Leeds the same facilities were given; the same price was required, and, soon after the promulgation of the arrangement, there was an addition of two hundred members to the ranks of the institution. And I may now remark, which I do with sincere pleasure, that the London School of Design has consented to give elementary drawing-books to all the Mechanics' Institutes which enter into the arrangements they have prescribed for the same. Already, I understand, there are drawing-classes established in twenty-seven institutions, and that the number of pupils therein is 682; and I cannot close the list of these various efforts and attractions which are displayed in the last year's labours of the Union, without being reminded that the Mechanics' Institute at Ripon has opened a commodious building for the purpose of carrying on, with increased facility, the various operations of that society. I am happy to find that my friend, the Very Reverend the Dean of Ripon, is here with us to-night, to give us an account of the spirit in which it is supported by those people who are happy enough to live under his presidency. In bringing before you these various details, I must enjoin upon all those who are here present, and may represent their several localities, to do all that in them lies to foster this wholesome spirit of competition and generous rivalry. Let us do what we can to communicate this electric impulse over all the varied features of our county's geography; let us speed it from mountain to valley; from forge and factory to meadow and to plough-land; from the manufacturing village that just lines the moor to the wateringplace that enlivens the sea-board; from Scarborough to Saddleworth, from Wensleydale to the Spurn; and in inviting your contemplations to these wholesome exercises of effort and of progress, I cannot help asking you just to contrast these emulations and this success — not in the spirit of undue conceit or selfsufficiency, but to contrast them on account of the gratitude they ought to inspire for the benefits which they have brought upon this land, with the evils which now prevail over too great a portion of the Continent of Europe. I say this, not with the idea of infringing the wholesome rule which excludes any party politics from our festivities and public celebrations, but with reference to those more general politics which decide the destinies of our species: let me ask you just to consider, in contrast with your own condition, the general aspect of affairs as presented to us among so many tribes and kindreds of the great European Continent. Why you yourselves, at Hull, probably, can only bear but too faithful witness to the embarrassments, the inconveniences, and the losses, which result from the blockade of friendly seas, fitted and purposed to receive and to interchange the commerce of the world; you yourselves can tell by the return of disconsolate vessels, how much harm is being inflicted by the blockade of the Elbe; by shutting the Sound; by the insensate hostilities between Germany and Denmark. But there is hardly a community which is not too disastrously suffering from the heavings of these revolutionary whirlwinds and storms. The Russians are on the Danube, the French are on the Tiber. It really seems as if the nations of Europe, in some species of wild bacchanal, were seizing the torches of civil discord and of foreign war, and throwing them, in their furious glee, from frontier to frontier, from river to river, from rampart to rampart, and scaring all the peaceful haunts of industry with their uncouth dissonance and hideous glare. While such are the appalling sights and sounds of which we catch the reflection, and hear the echo, here in Yorkshire, here in England, while we abide in our accustomed occupations, and move on in our allotted spheres, under the broad and equal light of freedom, let it be our care to kindle the genial lamp of knowledge, and to transmit it from hand to hand, from institute to institute, from wold to plain, from class to class, from the workshop to the cottage, over every portion of our land, till there shall be no dark corner unilluminated, till there shall be no haunt of obscene revelry unrebuked, till there shall be no abode of ignorance unenlightened, till there shall be no haunt of happy industry uncheered; and so, while we judge with all lowliness and humility of ourselves, we may become, in the judgment of the observing nations around us, and perhaps in the judgment of Him who judgeth not as man judgeth, a wise and understanding people.

YORKSHIRE UNION OF MECHANICS' INSTITUTES.
Leeds, June, 1851.

I HAVE sometimes felt inclined to remonstrate with my friends here for having led me to produce myself so frequently on these occasions, and, I may add, in this place. I might have thought that I had already inflicted enough in the way of lecture on the good people of Leeds, at least for some time to come; but I may be reminded that whatever may be my respect for them, this is not merely a town, or borough, or municipal meeting, but that it represents and constitutes an association which does not even confine itself to the boundaries of our wide West Riding, but enlarges its borders and stretches its stakes to the furthest limits of our entire county of York, and, I believe, even beyond it. With respect, too, to the time of our holding this assembly, it has been felt that this year of 1851, the first of this half-century, has, in many respects, been made a sort of Jubilee year, and that it behoves all good and laudable undertakings, and among them the Yorkshire Union of Mechanics' Institutes, to put on their best countenances, and summon the greatest number of their friends, and in all ways make much of themselves, not, I trust, for the purposes of a braggart and garish vanity, but for the sake of recommending what we really look upon as commendable in itself, and as calculated for extensive usefulness, to the widest possible amount of support and of imitation. All reasons these, however, the more why an old stager like myself should seek to make no undue trespass on your attention, but bear in his mind that we happily have to-night some new faces, as well as old to encourage; some new voices, as well as old, to instruct us. The Yorkshire Mechanics' Union can, indeed, no longer be regarded as an experiment; it is no sickly plant, no doubtful shoot, no fragile stem we have to rear, but it shows a robust and hardy trunk, and justly prides itself in its multitude of branches; comprising as it does, I believe, 117 institutions, and including within its branches, 20,000 members. No doubt the various delegates from the separate branches who have met to-day will have had the means of comparing the different methods and processes which have answered the best in the respective localities; this I take to be a principal advantage of these annual concourses; they afford an opportunity for comparison; they supply a whet-stone for emulation, not for envy; at the same time, 1 think it would be a mistake for each institution to consider itself bound to tread servilely in the track of every other; it is with these bodies as it is with nations at large; there will be a difference of circumstances, a difference of capabilities, a difference of humours. There are, of course, some broad rules and some obvious methods applicable to all; but, in the adaptation of them, the convenience, and the tastes, and the wants of the respective communities may be taken into consideration. There can be no better rule, (you must excuse me if I still find the echoes of Pope lingering about this room,)—

"Consult the genius of the place in all."

I naturally do not presume to enlarge upon details, which must have formed the subject of conference among the delegates this morning. A letter has been brought under my notice, written by Mr. Sikes, of Huddersfield, strongly urging the annexing of Savings' Banks to these institutions. Any step that would promote prudence and self-reliance is most deserving of consideration, but, as I have intimated, I consider any suggestion of this nature had better be left in the hands of those who have the practical management of the institutions. I have already adverted to the year 1851, and as there is extremely little I can say upon the general subject of Mechanics' Institutes which I have not, I fear but too often, before had opportunities of addressing to you, you will, I feel persuaded, make allowance for me, if, during the few minutes more I shall occupy of your time, I seek a variety from the ordinary topics of observation within that great Building, which some of you, I doubt not, have already seen, and all will have heard of, which gives to this year, 1851, now while it is gliding past us, and will probably give to it through all future time, its most distinguishing characteristic. Not that I am at all travelling out of the domain of Mechanics' Institutions when I refer to the Exhibition of 1851. Why say I this? Oh, enter for a moment with me through one of its many portals; stand under that lu id arch of glass, at the part where the broad transept intersects the far-stretching nave, while the summer sun glistens, first on the fresh young green of our forest elms, then on the tapering foliage of the tropics, then on the pale marble of the statuary, then on the thousand changing hues of the world's merchandise. I most truly believe that, as a mere spectacle, it surpasses any which the labour, and art, and power of man ever yet displayed in any one spot. Look at that long alley of plate, the stalls of goldsmiths and silversmiths; such a bright profusion was not spread out by Belshazzar when, amid the spoils of the Old Asia, he feasted his thousand lords. Examine the jewels and tissues of India, of Tunis, of Turkey; so dazzling an array was never piled behind the chariot of the Roman conqueror, when he led the long triumph up the hill of the Capitoline Jove;—observe the lustrous variety of porcelain, and tapestry, and silk, and bronze, and carving, which enters into the composition of furniture;—why Louis XIV. himself, could he be summoned from his grave, would confess that, although the French people had dethroned his dynasty, exiled his race, and obliterated that monarchy of which he was the special impersonation, they had carried all the arts of embellishment farther even than when he held his gorgeous court at Versailles. But I should not have obtruded these topics on an assembly like this, had I nothing to remark upon but the jewelled diadem, or the breathing brass, or the glistening marble, or the spangled brocade; these might only be fit adornments for the palaces of the great, or for the toilets of luxurious beauty; the title which the Crystal Palace of London has upon the suffrage of the judgment as well as the admiration of the eye, is, that it is the formal recognition of the value and dignity of labour—it is the throne and temple of industry;—industry and labour, in all their forms, as well as in all their climes, whether they are employed on the cheap gingham that makes up the wardrobe of the humblest cottager, or the richest lace that forms aprons for Queen or Cardinal—on the rude block from the quarry, and the hollow brick for model cottages. or the biggest diamond of the mine, the Mountain of Light itself; industry and labour, alike necessary to furnish their daily bread to the masses and the millions, and to embody in palpable form the brightest visions of poetry and art. Said I then wrong that this undertaking. thus intended and calculated to recognise and represent labour and industry, was not removed from the domain of Mechanics' Institutes? And when, further, I mark the space which is covered in this show-room of the world by the special industry of the West Riding of Yorkshire; when I recognise the banners which are suspended above the productions of your principal towns, with their, to me, most familiar devices—when I pass by, not without a sort of feeling of joint ownership—the woollens of Leeds, and stuffs of Bradford, and fancy goods of Huddersfield, and carpets of Halifax—(is their excellent and spirited manufacturer, Mr. Crossley, now among us?); and the hardware of Sheffield, and many other things from many other places, which I necessarily omit, to say nothing of all that wondrous, whirring machinery to which, among others, this town has contributed so conspicuously, I need offer no excuse for having connected the mechanics of Yorkshire with the Industrial Temple of 1851. One word of counsel to those who visit the Exhibition. It is divided, as you are probably aware, into two great sections, one belonging to our own empire, the other to the rest of the world. It had been anticipated, and it so turns out, that the British section shines most in what is solid, useful, practical, durable; in what is of most importance to the greatest numbers; while the Foreign section excels in brilliancy, in taste, in all that relates to decorative art; not that this line should be too rigidly drawn, for the Foreign division contains very much that is useful, and the British very much that is ornamental. What I would then earnestly advise every one, in his own branch of employment and skill, is, diligently to observe how, without foregoing what is valuable in his own workmanship, he can graft upon it whatever is attractive in that of others, and how, to the sterling home-bred qualities of use and durability, he may add the subtle charms of grace and beauty. This I would specially point out as an object of laudable ambition to your Schools of Design. And if I have ventured to offer one word of counsel to those who visit the Exhibition, let me conclude with one word of comfort to those whom circumstances may prevent from going there. Though I have described it justly as the most magnificent temple of industry, remember yet that the only worthy worship of industry must be carried on in the daily life and by the domestic hearth; this worship all have the power of rendering, and I can answer for it, there are two things more precious and bright even than any thing which is now displayed in the Crystal Palace,—the persevering energy of contented toil the sunny smile of an approving conscience.

MECHANICS' INSTITUTION.
Lincoln, October, 1851.

You have heard, ladies and gentlemen, that I have been named to move the first resolution, which I find runs thus: — " That Mechanics' Institutions, having for their object the advancement of the people in solid and useful education, deserve the support of all classes interested in the welfare of their common country." I find everything in the terms of that resolution to justify my recommending it to your cordial acceptance.

But, in offering a few brief observations in support of it, I feel that I ought to set out by making some sort of excuse to you for appearing here at all. It always seems to me upon such occasions as the present, that, except indeed in the neighbouring county of York, where I have got into the habit of doing as I am bid, I have no business to meddle with the concerns of other people. But, after all, it is not such a very long way across the Humber, and, on this occasion, I have acted under the special command of your excellent neighbour, the Earl of Yarborough. I know that he has performed the same good turn for the towns, I believe, both of Hull and of Sheffield; and I should be sorry to appear wanting in reciprocating any such neighbourly disposition. I feel, over and above all those local considerations, that the cause of Mechanics' Institutions is such as to justify any co-operation, no matter, however inefficient the person, or however remote his dwelling.

I must not forget, too, that I am a member of the Yorkshire Union of Mechanics' Institutions, an association which we think, in that county, has been of very considerable use in fostering the success of the institutions which are scattered within its borders. We understand that now for three or four years past the midland districts of our fair England have been desirous of being put under a system of equal efficiency and energy, and I feel that I may appear here once more as the representative of my old Yorkshire friends, to assure you that they heartily wish you success; and, if I know aright the feelings of those who have interested themselves in this cause, I am sure that they would hear of your complete success, even of your surpassing their own, with no other feeling but that of unalloyed satisfaction. And why should they not? England is no longer under the Heptarchy. The Humber, to which I have already referred, and "the smug and silvery Trent," as the world-wide poet (Shakspeare) calls it, no longer divides hostile and jealous regions. We may, it is true, some of us have our favourite boasts of what is to be found among ourselves. The Lincolnshire and Yorkshire wolds may contend with each other as to which are the best cultivated, without any great danger of being surpassed by any other portion of the kingdom. Young Grimsby may flatter itself that it may one day beat old Hull, and the palm of beauty may reasonably be contended for between the imposing masses of York Minster and the aspiring pinnacles of Lincoln Cathedral. But, as I have already hinted, the object which brings us together to-night is not a local one; it is scarcely a national one; it is a cosmopolitan one; for it aims at the progress of mankind and the advance of our species. Therefore, addressing you Midlanders, I say you are quite welcome to beat us of Yorkshire, if you can. If you fall short of us, we shall be willing to teach; and if you excel us, we shall be, I trust, docile to learn. There is no place from which one ought not to be content to pick up what is laudable and good. Why, when we look at the aspect of the midnight heavens, we are not so much struck with them when it is only a single star that twinkles athwart the gloom, but we most feel the beauty and the brightness, when all their boundless spaces are crowded with light, and when the stars, which may singly exceed each other in glory, collectively serve to show and set forth each other.

And this, I feel that I do not vainly flatter myself, will be the spirit of mankind at large when the civilisation of our race has attained its full developement. It may not be the era of a city like Athens, which absorbed into a single community an amount of poetry, of eloquence, of philosophy, and of art, unparalleled before or since; it may not be the era of an empire like Rome, which rolled up into itself all the eminence of the world; it may not be an era merely of splendid patronage or of surpassing discovery. No Shakspeare then may string the lyre, no Newton may measure the heavens; but it will be rather an era, when judicious enlightenment will pervade almost every community, and when liberal and refined accomplishments will distinguish almost every family. What I want you to feel, what I want you all, if any of you here have not joined it, to join such an institution as this for, is to make you feel how much each of you singly may do to aid this great consummation.

I know that the enemies of Mechanics' Institutes, and of popular institutions generally, have been apt to say that they have a tendency to make the mechanics and working men, whom especially they are intended to benefit, puffed up, presumptuous, conceited, and discontented. All I can say is, that if they do so, they fail singularly in their purpose, and fall far short of their aim. It appears to me that there are two principles upon which we must mainly rely for success in any attempts to raise and regenerate mankind. The one is to have a very high opinion of what we can do, the height to which we can soar, the advance in knowledge and in virtue which we may make,—that is, ambition as concerns our capacities. The other is to have a mean opinion of what we at any time know, or at any time have already done,—that is, humility as concerns our attainments. The ambition should be ever stirring us up to the even and steady development of righteous principles, and, where the opportunity presents itself, to the performance of noble, meritorious, and unselfish actions. The humility should ever keep in view that there is no sphere of life, however humble, no round of duties, however unexciting, which any of you may not enrich and elevate with qualities beside which the successes of statesmen and the triumphs of conquerors are but poor and vulgar. I believe there is no eminence to which man may not reach, but he must reach it by subordinating all unlawful impulses, and by subduing all mean ambitions. There is a general craving in the human mind for greatness and distinction. That greatness and distinction, I am thankful to think, is within the reach of any one to obtain ; but the greatness and distinction must not be without you, but within you.

I should be sorry to appear to take this opportunity of preaching what might be called a sermon, but I feel so fervid an interest in the welfare and progress of the great body of my countrymen, that I cannot refrain from enjoining them, even while I would invite them to a full enjoyment of all the rich resources and all the innocent pleasures of this our variegated world, never to lose hold of religion. I do not mean that you should necessarily confine it within those stiff and narrow grooves in which some would imprison its ethereal spirit; but I feel assured that it is the source among mankind of all that is large and all that is lovely, and that without it all would be dark and joyless. Under her sacred wing you may securely resign yourselves to all that is improving in knowledge, or instructing in science, or captivating in art, or beautiful in nature. The Architect of the Universe, the Author of Being, such as Christianity represents Him, cannot but approve of every creature that He has made developing to the utmost extent the faculties He has given him, and examining, in all its depth and mystery, every work of His hand. Shut up the page of knowledge and the sources of enjoyment from the multitude, because some have occasionally abused the blessed privilege! Why, the very same argument would consign every man and woman to a cloister, because the world and active life are full of traps and pitfalls. No. Pre-eminent and supreme as I am convinced religion is, yet to make her so in the convictions and hearts of men, I feel she must discard all timidity, must front every truth in the full blaze of light, and sympathise with every pursuit and every impulse of our race.

I have thus briefly shadowed forth the reasons why no person ought to frown upon Mechanics' Institutions. I do not wish to attribute to them any exaggerated or imaginary value; I do not hold them forth as singly containing the elements with which we should hope to regenerate modern society; but it is because I believe them calculated happily to chime in with the existing wants and prevailing dispositions of the times, to afford opportunities for improvement and development in quarters where they would not otherwise be found, to promote innocent recreation and blameless amusements, and generally to assist the progress of mankind, that I thus venture to recommend them to your cordial sympathy and your active assistance.

BURNLEY MECHANICS' INSTITUTE.
November, 1851.

LADIES AND GENTLEMEN—
I thank you from my heart for the very generous reception which you have given to one who has yet certainly been a stranger to the town of Burnley. But you, sir, have just carried me back into Yorkshire, and it is certainly true that, across the hills which rise just above your town, I have had many opportunities of addressing audiences upon similar occasions in some of those valleys which, like your own, are distinguished alike by the beauties of their natural scenery and by the busy hum of human

industry. And I feel that in coming before a Lancashire audience we are no longer living in the times, so eloquently adverted to by a late speaker, when the names of York and Lancaster signified different factions and parties; but now, on the contrary, we are in a happier era, when either your red rose has paled, or our white rose has blushed, into one common colour, and instead of contending for rival causes or for opposing dynasties, we may now only try to boast among each other which has the most or the best supported and best conducted Mechanics' Institutions. I have had many occasions heretofore, and very recent ones, of remarking upon the singular elasticity of these Mechanics' Institutions, I mean their adaptation to the varied aspects of our society. Scarcely a month ago, I attended at a similar meeting in the city of Lincoln, an old and picturesquely built town, the capital of the most agricultural district in England; the towers of whose majestic cathedral look down from their lofty perch upon a wide expanse of reclaimed fens and level corn fields: and among that agricultural population, under the shade of that old cathedral, a thriving Mechanics' Institution has been established. And now I find myself in Burnley, one of that cluster of busy manufacturing towns and communities, which stud this district of England, like the broad brazen knobs upon some old belt. It may be true that their names are not surrounded with the halo of classical or romantic associations. The names of Bolton, and Blackburn, and Bury, and Bacup, and Burnley, have not the imposing and picturesque sound either of Thebes, or Corinth, or Argos, in ancient Greece; or of Padua, or Mantua, or Verona, in modern Italy. But they have at least this comparative advantage, they are not marching their inhabitants in trained bands to batter down each other's walls and assault each other's citizens; their contention, if contention there is among them, is in the pursuits of a peaceful industry, and if they are at strife with each other, it is upon the equal field of honourable enterprise, where all the laurels which are won serve both to crown themselves and to enrich the whole population. Now in a place and district like this, I consider a Mechanics' Institution to be a most appropriate appendage; and therefore it is with great pleasure that I found myself enabled to take part in the auspicious proceedings of this morning. And when I say it is an appropriate appendage, I feel that I understate the truth; it is a most desirable and almost indispensable one. I have just referred to the nature of the pursuits which are followed here as being peaceful and useful and honourable, but at the same time we must not forget that primarily and in themselves they are conversant only with what is material and with the ways (to use a homely phrase) of making money; and that they might have a tendency, if unchecked and unbalanced by anything in an opposite direction, to engross and enchain some of the more delicate tastes, or the loftier aspirations of the human mind. Far be it from me, in Lancashire or anywhere else, to speak slightingly of cotton; but you must feel that cotton and calico, though they make admirable stockings and other equally indispensable articles of clothing, yet do not in themselves furnish out the whole man. Now, I have observed that a most accomplished and able person, whom I may call a fellow lecturer of my own, Dr. Lyon Playfair, in an address he recently delivered, gave it as his opinion with respect to the modes of education pursued in this country, that in our schools and colleges enough attention has not been given to scientific instruction and regular industrial training. He complains that too much labour may have been bestowed on classical studies, on dead authors, on by-gone poets, and that the faculties have not been enough exercised on the open page of nature and the living wonders which are around and about and above and beneath us. Now, I think that he is probably in the right in this, but at the same time I am convinced that almost every prevailing direction, both of the individual mind and of society at large, ought occasionally to have administered to it something in the way of reaction and of corrective. It may be very well, in the quiet of academic bowers, that the dim cloisters of Oxford and the still shades of Cambridge, retaining, as I hope they ever will do, their old appropriate sources of learning, not ignoring (to use a modern phrase, which I might probably be told in those classic precincts was a barbarous one) the accustomed voices of their own Muses, should yet reflect more, as I believe they have begun to do, of the aspect of the century and the society in which they are placed. But on the other hand, in a district like this, where the pursuit of wealth is the habitual rule, where the recurring routine of labour is the daily life, where the steam engine and the power loom and mechanism and machinery seem to be the lords of time and space, of the body and of the mind, it is well too, that without neglecting, on the contrary while you are directly encouraging, those subjects of inquiry which are congenial to the place, while you are promoting the study of the law of nature and inquiring into the properties of matter, at the same time the means of access should be given, and opportunities for a hearing at least, afforded, to the claims of general literature, the sober muse of history, the fervid accents of oratory, and the sublime inspirations of song. And just as it is the boast of our country, England, that it is the self-same country which produced her Newton, who has laid down the positive and ascertained laws of other worlds and other systems, and her Shakspeare, whose imagination peopled worlds almost as numerous, and quite as bright; just as those mingling character-istics still in some sort distinguish our countrymen, at once the most sober-minded and adventurous race which the world has known; so let it be the aim and glory of our own times, on the one hand, to make the study of the recluse and the vigil of the student still more available for the wants of the present day, and for obtaining a mastery over nature, still more useful, still more practical, than they have yet been ; so, on the other hand, we should aim to throw around the dreary monotony of toil, and the plodding perseverance of labour, charms and graces which are not their own. And for these reasons I rejoice, again, that such an institution as has already existed here, it is now proposed to ex-tend, to diffuse, to embody in a more worthy home ; I rejoice to hear that it is proposed to combine with it lecture-rooms, classes for drawing and for music and for languages, together with a well assorted library ; and that it is purposed not to be wanting in the graces of external architecture ; and I trust that you will show yourselves alive to the occasion which opens itself thus before you, and that when the effort has been made, and the brick and mortar, —I beg your pardon, for I believe you have excellent stone of your own in Burnley, — when all this is brought together, and a goodly edifice is raised, you will show that it has the support of the in-habitants, and that the intelligence and mind which have to be developed within it will make the real glory of that building. I know that when I address you in Lancashire, I am among a com-munity which has shown a great and growing interest in the cause of popular education in all its directions. Into the merits of any particular direction which that interest may assume, this is not the place or opportunity to enter. But I feel it a real triumph to think that the time has come when the education of the people must spread wide and strike deep, and I have faith that the wisdom and the public spirit of all classes in this country will be guided to give that impulse a right direction. Of a truth there is something large and expansive in the bodies of men which in this portion of the country are brought together upon an occasion like the present. Why, in the very place * in which we are assembled, in the very person † who laid the first stone of your new building, we have living and patent proof that there is nothing exclusive or repelling in the assistance and energy which are brought to bear upon it. And as I have referred to Mechanics' Institutions as comprising in their range the cathedral towers of Lincoln and the factories of Burnley, so I have seen to-day that they may unite in their service the oldest and most ancestral modes of faith, and the least fettered and least hierarchical forms. From my heart I join in the wish, which I feel sure will be entertained by all who have now been brought together, and which has already found an expression in the mouths of preceding speakers, that the Institution of which, amid so many demonstrations of good will and concord, the first stone has been laid this day, and of which we are now holding this commemorative assembly, may in its future development, never suffer those whom it may bring within its walls, or who may be partakers of its benefits, to derive any influence that is inconsistent with their duties as good citizens, good subjects, good men, good Christians — that they may under its roof find much to instruct, much to amuse, much to refine, much to elevate; — nothing to corrupt, nothing to sully, nothing to sap the wholesome foundation of morals or impair the sacred principles of religion; but that while they may continue to enjoy the opportunities it affords for useful instruction and for rational recreation, they may at the same time be imbibing lessons which shall stimulate and sweeten their daily toil, and make their own homes and firesides honest and happy.

* The Independent Chapel. † Charles Towneley, Esq. of Towneley.

THE END.

LONDON : PRINTED BY SPOTTISWOODE & CO. NEW-STREET SQUARE

www.ingramcontent.com/pod-product-compliance
Lightning Source LLC
Chambersburg PA
CBHW020112170426
43199CB00009B/498